T0358428

FOREIGN TRADE IN THE CENTRALLY PLANNED ECONOMY

FUNDAMENTALS OF PURE AND APPLIED ECONOMICS

EDITORS IN CHIEF

J. LESOURNE, Conservatoire National des Arts et Métiers, Paris, France

H. SONNENSCHEIN, University of Pennsylvania, Philadelphia, PA, USA

ADVISORY BOARD

K. ARROW, Stanford, CA, USA
W. BAUMOL, Princeton, NJ, USA
W. A. LEWIS, Princeton, NJ, USA
S. TSURU, Tokyo, Japan

ECONOMIC SYSTEMS & COMPARATIVE ECONOMICS II
In 3 Volumes

FOREIGN TRADE IN THE CENTRALLY PLANNED ECONOMY

THOMAS A WOLF

First published in 1988 by
Harwood Academic Publishers GmbH

Reprinted in 2001 by
Routledge
2 Park Square, Milton Park, Abingdon, Oxon, OX14 4RN

Transferred to Digital Printing 2007

Routledge is an imprint of the Taylor & Francis Group

© 1988 Harwood Academic Publishers GmbH

The publishers have made every effort to contact authors/copyright holders
of the works reprinted in *Harwood Fundamentals of Pure & Applied Economics*.
This has not been possible in every case, however, and we would welcome
correspondence from those individuals/companies we have been unable to
trace.

These reprints are taken from original copies of each book. in many cases
the condition of these originals is not perfect. the publisher has gone to
great lengths to ensure the quality of these reprints, but wishes to point
out that certain characteristics of the original copies will, of necessity, be
apparent in reprints thereof.

British Library Cataloguing in Publication Data
A CIP catalogue record for this book
is available from the British Library

Foreign Trade in the Centrally Planned Economy
ISBN 0-415-27469-9
Economic Systems & Comparative Economics II: 3 Volumes
ISBN 0-415-26963-6
Harwood Fundamentals of Pure & Applied Economics
ISBN 0-415-26907-5

Foreign Trade in the Centrally Planned Economy

Thomas A. Wolf
International Monetary Fund, Washington, DC, USA

A volume in the Economic Systems section
edited by
J. M. Montias
Yale University, USA

 harwood academic publishers
chur· london paris · new york · melbourne

© 1988 by Harwood Academic Publishers GmbH
Poststrasse 22, 7000 Chur, Switzerland
All rights reserved

Harwood Academic Publishers

Post Office Box 197
London WC2E 9PX
England

58, rue Lhomond
75005 Paris
France

Post Office Box 786
Cooper Station
New York, NY 10276
United States of America

Private Bag 8
Camberwell, Victoria 3124
Australia

Library of Congress Cataloging-in-Publication Data

Wolf, Thomas A.
  Foreign trade in the centrally planned economy.

  (Fundamentals of pure and applied economics,
ISSN 0191-1708; vol. 27. Economic systems section)
  Bibliography: p.
  Includes index.
  1. International trade. 2. Economic policy.
3. Balance of trade. I. Title. II. Series:
Fundamentals of pure and applied economics; vol. 27.
III. Series: Fundamentals of pure and applied
economics. Economic systems section.
HF1411.W582   1988   382   87-37840
ISBN 3-7186-4813-X

Contents

To my mother

Dorothy Downing Wolf

Introduction to the Series

Drawing on a personal network, an economist can still relatively easily stay well informed in the narrow field in which he works, but to keep up with the development of economics as a whole is a much more formidable challenge. Economists are confronted with difficulties associated with the rapid development of their discipline. There is a risk of "balkanization" in economics, which may not be favorable to its development.

Fundamentals of Pure and Applied Economics has been created to meet this problem. The discipline of economics has been subdivided into sections (listed inside). These sections include short books, each surveying the state of the art in a given area.

Each book starts with the basic elements and goes as far as the most advanced results. Each should be useful to professors needing material for lectures, to graduate students looking for a global view of a particular subject, to professional economists wishing to keep up with the development of their science, and to researchers seeking convenient information on questions that incidentally appear in their work.

Each book is thus a presentation of the state of the art in a particular field rather than a step-by-step analysis of the development of the literature. Each is a high-level presentation but accessible to anyone with a solid background in economics, whether engaged in business, government, international organizations, teaching, or research in related fields.

Three aspects of *Fundamentals of Pure and Applied Economics* should be emphasized:

—First, the project covers the whole field of economics, not only theoretical or mathematical economics.

—Second, the project is open-ended and the number of books is not predetermined. If new interesting areas appear, they will generate additional books.

—Last, all the books making up each section will later be grouped to constitute one or several volumes of an Encyclopedia of Economics.

The editors of the sections are outstanding economists who have selected as authors for the series some of the finest specialists in the world.

J. Lesourne   *H. Sonnenschein*

Abbreviations

CPE	Centrally planned economy
CMEA	Council for Mutual Economic Assistance
FTO	Foreign trade organization
GDP	Gross domestic product
LDC	Less developed country
ME	Market economy
MFT	Ministry of Foreign Trade
MPE	Modified planned economy
TR	Transferable ruble

Foreign Trade in the Centrally Planned Economy

THOMAS A. WOLF

International Monetary Fund, Washington DC, USA

1. INTRODUCTION

The centrally planned economy (CPE) considered in this mono-graph is a stylized version of the planned economies actually existing in the Soviet Union and, beginning in the late 1940s and early 1950s, in most of Eastern Europe. This essay is therefore neither an examination of foreign trade in a hypothetical CPE,[1] an exposition of the Marxian theory of foreign trade, nor a study of the implicit role that foreign trade might play in the so-called Lange-Lerner model or other models of market socialism. Rather, the objective of this essay is to explore the ways in which the main features of this stylized real-world CPE influence, along with the internal and external environment, its foreign trade behavior and the level and pattern of its trade.

Because the CPE examined in this study is a stylized repre-sentation of real-world economies, it is not always easy to distin-guish between the *systemic* and *policy* determinants of its foreign trade behavior and outcomes.[2] Whenever possible such distinctions are made here, but because in most instances foreign trade behavior is in fact co-determined by both factors, and they are both very difficult to quantify, it is usually impossible to separate out their different effects. By necessity, therefore, the CPE portrayed in this

---

[1] Foreign trade behavior of a hypothetical CPE that follows Pareto-optimal rules is examined in Batra [7]. A critique, which emphasizes the differences between this hypothetical CPE and those existing in the real world, is provided by Wolf [122].

[2] The theoretical framework that distinguishes among an economy's environment, system, goals, policies and outcomes is developed in Koopmans and Montias [61] and Montias [84]. An application of this framework to CPE foreign trade is provided by Hewett [42].

study is a centrally planned economy with a specific set of fundamental policies, a set which has been heavily influenced by the historical environment in which the CPE was established and developed. A CPE could be imagined, of course, in which policymakers operated with a very different policy configuration, which in general would result in very different foreign trade behavior and outcomes; as noted, however, such a "hypothetical" CPE is not discussed in this essay.

The second section briefly describes the organization of foreign trade activities in the CPE, and discusses the main institutional and policy determinants of CPE foreign trade behavior. The actual impact that these factors have on foreign trade decisionmaking is examined in more detail in Section 3. The role of foreign trade in the macroeconomy and in macroeconomic stabilization in the CPE is the focus of the fourth section. Because there are continuing efforts in a number of real-world CPEs to improve economic performance through economic reforms, Section 5 examines in some detail the pressures for reform that emerge in foreign trade as well as the impact that reform may have on foreign trade decision-making and macroeconomic adjustment in the "modified" CPE.

2. INSTITUTIONAL AND POLICY CONTEXT

The economic system of the real-world CPE has the following characteristics that are directly relevant to the conduct of foreign trade: state ownership of the bulk of the means of production; information flows and hierarchical bargaining over enterprise plans and access to resources, which occur in a bureaucratic rather than a market environment; the elaboration of detailed central plans for enterprise inputs and outputs; rigid prices set by the central authorities, which are intended to facilitate the planning process and the evaluation of enterprise performance; plan fulfillment, rather than profits, as the main criterion for evaluation; a relatively free labor market, but wages that are subject to close regulation from the center; and a monolithic state banking system that passively supplies the credit necessary to physical plan fulfillment and that maintains a fairly strict dichotomy between the money supplies held by enterprises and households, respectively.

The authorities in real-world CPEs have typically adopted the following fundamental policy objectives: rapid industrialization, based on a high rate of capital accumulation and a rapid growth rate of the industrial labor force; retail price stability; downward rigidity in money wages; full employment and indeed individual job security; and strict limits on wage and salary differentials (on the prototype CPE system, see Campbell [27] and Nove [90]).

In this CPE, foreign trade is largely carried out by a number of state-owned foreign trade organizations (FTOs) that are mainly subordinate to the Ministry of Foreign Trade (MFT).[3] The MFT is subordinate, in turn, to the governmental Council of Ministers. Generally the FTOs only engage in foreign trade, and do not have manufacturing operations or distribute goods domestically at the wholesale or retail level. Although in some cases the industrial branch ministries, also subordinate to the Council of Ministers, may have some direct influence on the activities of the FTOs, for the most part these ministries and the domestic trading and/or producing enterprises under their authority have little direct relationship with foreign enterprises. The FTOs generally are non-competing with one another, and therefore each FTO may be considered to have a foreign trade monopoly for a particular range of products. Likewise, the FTOs together, and by the same token their principal superior organ, the MFT, constitute an institutional state monopoly of foreign trade.

Annual and five-year plans for foreign trade are developed as the result of a bargaining process involving the provision by the FTOs of information on foreign market developments, the aggregation of the draft plans of individual FTOs by the MFT, and the development of both disaggregated and aggregated plans by the governmental Central Planning Commission, in close coordination with the supreme political authorities and the individual branch ministries responsible for domestic production and domestic trade. The foreign trade plan that emerges from a process of several iterations is an integral part of the overall national economic plan. It specifies, in varying degrees of detail, the volume, commodity composition and geographical pattern of foreign trade that is to be undertaken in the next period. The aggregate plan for imports essentially reflects the pattern of the central planners' excess demands, after taking

---

[3] In reality the patterns of authority with respect to foreign trade are often somewhat more complex. See Gardner [35] and Gruzinov [36].

into account domestic production objectives, for those goods that are central to plan fulfillment in priority sectors. Exports, on the other hand, are planned for the most part in light of the foreign exchange needs implied by the import plan and a balance of payments constraint. Most imports and exports are reflected in the so-called material balances worked out by the planners, which may cover hundreds or even several thousands of material inputs that are deemed critical for overall plan fulfillment.[4]

Institutional determinants of foreign trade behavior

The foregoing institutional set-up has several distinctive implications for foreign trade behavior and outcomes in the CPE. First, the state monopoly of foreign trade institutionally separates, and indeed insulates, domestic producers and consumers from foreign markets. As a result, domestic producers of both exportables and importables tend to be insulated from competitive forces on world markets, and their standards for quality and innovation in production and for reliability in delivery are largely determined by those of the domestic market. This insulation from the world market is manifested most clearly in the difficulty that CPEs have in exporting finished and, in many cases, even semi-finished manufactures to market economies (MEs).

Second, the predominance of bureaucratic, or vertical relationships over horizontal relationships with other enterprises, and the tendency for firms to concentrate their dealings with other enterprises belonging to the same ministry, has the effect of limiting the degree of specialization, particularly in final products. This, in turn, restricts the degree to which FTOs have been able to base their export strategies on specialization within the realm of manufactures, and their ability to attain and maintain strong positions on the highly competitive export markets for manufactured products in MEs (Winiecki (121)).

Third, the *de facto* predominant role played by quantity targets in the plans of both domestic enterprises and the FTOs, together with managerial remuneration schemes tied mainly to plan fulfillment,

---

[4] For in-depth descriptions of the organization of the foreign trade sector in the CPEs, see Pryor [96], Hewett [41], Gruzinov [36], and Gardner [35].

result in an extraordinary emphasis being placed by the CPE on the quantity of production rather than its quality. This emphasis spills over into foreign trade, as well, and is a further cause of the relative difficulty that CPEs have in exporting to MEs those manufactures that are subject to significant product differentation on the basis of quality (Holzman [47]).

A fourth crucial determinant of CPE foreign trade behavior is the domestic price system taken together with the incentive system and the very limited degree of autonomy enjoyed by the FTOs. Domestic prices at the producers' and wholesale level are administratively fixed, by the State Price Office, and typically held constant for long periods. Although fixed prices may reflect important policy objectives, in this case they can also be viewed as the logical outcome of central planning. The fixing of prices facilitates the planners' tasks of aggregation across thousands or millions of commodities, and it also simplifies the evaluation of enterprise performance in the sense that with fixed prices, enterprise revenues and costs can easily be given a physical as well as a value interpretation. Moreover, it removes from the State Price Office the burden of attempting to simulate market outcomes for the thousands or millions of individual products.

For accounting purposes the foreign currency values of traded goods are converted at a so-called *valuta* or external exchange rate into a "foreign exchange" equivalent of the local currency (e.g., foreign exchange rubles, or *valuta* rubles). This accounting unit will typically not be directly convertible by FTOs into domestic currency (Pryor [96]). Unlike domestic prices, foreign currency prices will generally be subject to frequent change. Even if the valuta exchange rate is fixed, the valuta value of the trade of a FTO, and of the aggregate value of the CPE's exports and imports, will fluctuate along with changes in foreign currency prices as well as with changes in trade volumes. Abstracting from FTO commissions and overhead costs, the FTOs as a group earn a profit (T) from foreign trade equal to:

$$T = Q_m(P_m - P_m^* e') + Q_x(P_x^* e' - P_x), \qquad (1)$$

where Q_m and Q_x represent the volumes of a composite import and export, respectively, P_m is the weighted average price at which FTOs resell imports to domestic trading organizations, P_x is the weighted average price at which FTOs purchase exports from domestic producers, P_m^* and P_x^* are the weighted average foreign currency prices of imports and exports, respectively, and e' is the *valuta* exchange rate, expressed in units of the nominal valuta currency per unit of foreign exchange. The valuta value of imports and exports will be equal to $P_m' Q_m$ and $P_x' Q_x$, respectively, where $P_m' = P_m^* e'$ and $P_x' = P_x^* e'$. The foreign trade profit of the FTOs is only nominal from their standpoint, because it is exactly offset (ignoring commissions) by a system of so-called *price equalization* taxes (if $T_i > 0$) and subsidies (if $T_i < 0$), where T_i refers to the net profit on price discrepancies earned by the ith FTO (Pryor [96], Wiles [120] and Wolf [124]).

Unless an FTO has market power in foreign markets, the foreign currency prices it faces, as well as the administratively set domestic prices, are beyond its control. Its import plan will typically be fixed in volume terms, for these goods will mainly be high priority goods critical to fulfillment of the national economic plan. If FTO commissions, and in turn the remuneration of its employees, are a function of its nominal profit or the extent to which this profit exceeds planned profit, the enterprise may have an incentive to search for the lowest cost sources of foreign supply of the specified imports. Because the volume constraint is binding, however, the FTO's effective negotiating room, in the event it has external market power, will be limited.

On the export side, the autonomy of the FTO *vis-à-vis* the higher authorities may be somewhat greater. This is because the FTO itself is in a position to identify and analyze changing export prospects, and unlike in the case of imports it will not face a centrally imposed minimum constraint on its export volumes. If it could obtain a higher price by cutting back its export offer, and still earn the valuta revenue called for in the plan, it might be evaluated just that much more highly, as this action would free additional quantities of the exportable for domestic consumption. If the FTO were instead evaluated mainly with respect to its nominal profit, T, then it would seek to equate its marginal revenue from exporting with the marginal cost of this activity. If it also had external market power, this would imply setting its export price above the fixed domestic price it pays for the exportable. If instead it were a price taker abroad, the profit maximizing FTO would attempt to maximize its export volume, given the fixed domestic price of the exportable. If revenue maximization were the objective of the FTO, it would try to maximize export volume if it were a price taker, but would attempt to set its export price to correspond with the unit elastic point on its foreign demand curve if it enjoyed external market power.

Although greater autonomy may exist on the export side, it is usually considered that FTOs in practice have only limited autonomy in the CPE. To give FTOs a significant degree of autonomy would, after all, work against the fundamental objective of central planning, which is to exert the maximum possible central control over all areas of resource allocation. As a result, the overall "offer curve" of the CPE is likely to be decided at the level of the central authorities, and to be determined by aggregate economic considerations rather than by the parochial concerns of individual FTOs (see Section 3).[5]

A fifth consideration is that this circumscribed autonomy of the FTOs and the insulation of domestic enterprises from foreign markets will logically be reinforced by a policy of *de jure* resident inconvertibility with respect to the purchase and sale of foreign exchange. Importing FTOs must apply to the Ministry of Finance or the state-owned Foreign Trade Bank for the foreign exchange needed to meet their plans. Only in rare circumstances would domestic persons or enterprises be allowed to purchase foreign exchange (for example, in the case of authorized trips abroad, and so forth). Exporting FTOs typically will not earn foreign exchange; rather, their revenues denominated in foreign currencies will be paid directly to the above-mentioned financial authorites, which will offset these revenues with valuta earnings credited to the FTOs' bank accounts.

Sixth, the centralized formulation and implementation of foreign trade plans has a subtle but powerful impact on the *de facto* convertibility of a CPE's currency. Because all intermediate and final investment products are centrally allocated, and since all trade by the FTOs is in principle stipulated in their plans, by volume and assortment, there is very little unplanned trade. Now consider a

---

[5] Indirect evidence for the central determination of the effective offer curve of the CPE is provided in Wolf [127].

foreign firm that exports to the CPE. It could take payment in some convertible currency; or, if it is based in a member country of the regional grouping of the CPEs, the Council for Mutual Economic Assistance (CMEA), it could accept a claim in its domestic currency or valuta at its own national bank, which in turn would increase its own claim on the importing CPE in terms of the common intra-CMEA clearing unit, the transferable ruble (TR).[6] Alternatively, at least in theory, the foreign exporter could accept in payment a direct claim on the banking system of the CPE. Because the importing CPE's exports in the present and possibly even in foreseeable plan periods have already been largely determined, however, the foreign holder of its currency would be severely limited in terms of the domestic purchasing power of this currency. For this reason, and independent of whatever legal restrictions might be applied to the exchange of the CPE's currency for others (including, as noted above, resident inconvertibility), its currency may be said to lack "commodity convertibility," and therefore will be *de facto* inconvertible for nonresidents, at least for large purchases (Holzman [47, 52]). In general, foreign enterprises will not want to hold the CPE's currency, except insofar as they must meet the local costs of doing business in this economy.[7] In trade with market economies, most transactions not involving some type of barter operation will therefore be settled in the convertible currencies of the MEs. With other CPEs, most trade will be settled in TRs.

Finally, a certain degree of "trade aversion" may be a natural concomitant of central planning (Brown [24]). Specifically, an important rationale for the establishment of the CPE and its institutions is to give the planners the ability to insulate the domestic economy as much as possible against the vagaries of world market forces. Even if the planners could easily and precisely calculate the CPE's comparative advantages in the international marketplace (for reasons why this is difficult, see Section 3), they might be unwilling to expand trade to the extent suggested by the

---

[6] On the CMEA in general, see Kaser [59], Marer and Montias [75], and van Brabant [115]. The payments systems within the CMEA are discussed by Allen [1] and Brainard [23]. In 1987 the members of the CMEA were Bulgaria, Cuba, Czechoslovakia, the German Democratic Republic (East Germany), Hungary, Mongolia, Poland, Romania, the Soviet Union, and Viet Nam.

[7] For an exception to this general rule, see the discussion later in this section.

familiar Pareto-optimal conditions for fear that this level of trade and degree of specialization would raise too high the risk of nonfulfillment of the national economic plan, given the uncertainties of world markets. We would therefore expect, *ceteris paribus*, a CPE to have a less specialized production and trade structure and a lower level of foreign trade relative to its national income, than an otherwise comparable market economy (Boltho [12] and Winiecki [121]). The perceived trade aversion of CPEs is also frequently attributed to a *policy* of import substitution; to some degree this is justified, because in addition to being biased away from trade and specialization by the logic of central planning itself, CPEs have often adopted a policy of relative self-sufficiency for other reasons (Pryor [96], Kaser [59] and Wiles [120]).

Policy determinants of foreign trade behavior

Price rigidity at the producers level was earlier observed to be partly a logical outcome of the choice of central planning—it facilitates the authorities' planning and evaluation tasks. To a lesser degree, a commitment to retail price stability in the CPEs could be explained on similar grounds. Much more important in the case of retail prices, however, and of some significance as well in the case of producers' prices, is the fixing of prices for long periods as a matter of policy rather than simply as the handmaiden of central planning.

To some extent, and particularly in the earliest years of central planning, the decision administratively to set rigid prices was based on ideological grounds—the rigidity and, to some extent, arbitrariness of prices was viewed as a healthy manifestation of the repeal, under socialism, of the so-called Law of Value (Nove [90]). At the retail level, however, fixed prices also reflect two policy preoccupations of the authorities in realworld CPEs—the desire for macro- and micro-level price stability, so as to avoid both inflation and the uncertainties of price fluctuations, and the concern that all individuals in society be able to afford to consume basic necessities in at least adequate quantities.

To accommodate these social policy goals, the retail price structure is established largely independently of the price structure faced by producers and wholesalers. The independence of the two price structures is maintained through a system of differentiated turnover taxes. Consequently, whereas the level and structure of producer and wholesale prices are insulated from the level and structure of world market prices by the system of price equalization, retail prices in turn are insulated from wholesale prices by the differentiated turnover taxes. Moreover, because neither of the domestic price structures is meant in general to be market-clearing nor to reflect the underlying marginal costs of production, neither structure reflects the relative scarcities of the economy.

One implication of this "arbitrariness" of the domestic price structures is that the planners, who in general are responsible for deciding the volume and pattern of foreign trade, are not able to use the level or the structure of domestic prices, relative to world market prices, as a reliable guide to comparative advantage (see Boltho [12] and the references therein). A second implication is that the level and structure of domestic prices are not a reliable guide for establishing the prices at which the FTOs should engage in foreign trade. The result, as discussed in greater detail in Section 3, is that CPEs must even use world prices as a basis (to which various agreed-upon adjustments are made) for their mutal trade.

A further consequence of the rigidity of domestic prices is that short- and medium-run adjustment to exogenous disturbances, whether or not originating in foreign trade, will be largely in terms of changes in quantities rather than in prices of goods and services. In other words, the system of official prices in the CPE does not serve as a transmission belt for economic disturbances or as a signalling device for adjustment to such disturbances.

Finally, the distortion in general of domestic prices from both world market prices and the structure of real production costs domestically may lead the authorities to impose an upper legal limit on the *nonresident* convertibility of the domestic currency. This is because, as an exception to the general *de facto* commodity inconvertibility of the currency mentioned earlier, the consumption (as opposed to the production) of most consumer goods is not enforced by the central authorities in the CPE. While domestic consumers may not possess "consumer sovereignty," they do have a choice, subject to their own budget constraints and the actual availability of goods on the domestic market, about which products and in what quantities they wish to consume. To forestall, say, large-scale purchases by foreign arbitrageurs of domestically produced consumer goods at the retail level, which would then be sold abroad at a profit (possibly after being bought on the domestic market at a price below the real domestic cost of production), the authorities may well impose a ceiling on the amount of domestic currency that foreigners can buy (Holzman [47]).

A second policy objective of real-world CPEs, after price stability and indeed the rigidity of individual prices, has been the strategy of rapid industrialization and economic growth. In this sense the CPE is very much a "priority economy" (Brown and Neuberger [26]). One (not necessary) consequence of the growth priority has been the underpricing of capital goods, at least insofar as enterprises are effectively spared an interest charge on the use of capital. Some have argued that the underpricing of capital has reinforced the tendency to over-produce capital-intensive relative to labor-intensive goods in the CPEs. It is further argued that this would help explain the emerging Leontief paradox in CPE trade (at least in the 1960s), evidence for which was a shift by CPEs (many of which are poorly endowed in natural resources, the exploitation of which is normally quite capital intensive) from a capital-intensive import bias to a capital-intensive export bias in trade with the relatively capital-abundant developed market economies (Rosefielde [97, 99], Gardner [35] and Winiecki [121]). In an economy that relies relatively so little on price incentives, however, it is not clear how important a role relative prices *per se* have had in influencing resource allocation, in comparison with administratively directed resource flows which have tended to favor goods over services, industry over agriculture, and within industry, heavy industry over light. In any event, reflecting these priorities, the CPEs tend to have a commodity structure of both exports and imports that is relatively heavily weighted toward capital goods and relatively capital-intensive industrial raw materials and semi-processed goods, in trade with both the MEs and with other planned economies.[8]

Yet a third basic policy orientation commonly thought to have a major impact on foreign trade behavior and outcomes is "overly taut planning" or "over-full employment planning" (Holzman

---

[8] The formal empirical evidence with respect to the differences between the composition of CPE and ME trade, respectively, is not as unambiguous, however, as one might expect. For a review of such evidence, see Hewett [42]; also see Montias [85].

[44, 47] and Hunter [58]). In principle, of course, there is no reason why planners should adopt plans that overstate the economy's productive possibilities. This tendency, seen particularly in the early years of central planning, appears to have derived from a perception at the center that the adoption of an overly ambitious plan would result in higher aggregate output, at least in the priority sectors, than would occur were the plan more consistent and less ambitious.

Even when domestic excess demand for resources in the CPE is not consciously planned, it may still result from an over-bidding for investment goods and construction materials in the event that the industrial ministries and the enterprises perceive that they will be best rewarded for output-maximizing behavior that will not be curtailed, at least over the medium term, by strict financial discipline. This excess demand, sometimes referred to as the "suction" of the market, has several implications for foreign trade.[9]

One implication is that exports will be viewed by all levels of the economic hierarchy as directly depriving domestic economic agents of resources. Planners may see exports as essentially a "necessary evil" in the production, through foreign trade, of the imports critical to plan fulfillment. Lacking will be a genuine microeconomic interest in exports which, unlike in the market economy, will not be prized for generating employment or profits, because full employment is mandated in the CPE and most enterprises exist in a sellers' market domestically. For this reason CPEs are unlikely to launch sustained export drives to capture new markets in the MEs, or to be particularly aggressive in protecting their market positions, once established (Holzman [47, 48] and Winiecki [121]).

Another implication of the domestic sellers' market will be a relative lack of concern for quality, packaging and reliability of export deliveries, which together will reinforce the above-mentioned tendencies against being competitive on world markets, particularly in manufactures (Holzman [47]). Generalized excess demand pressures will inevitably also lead to domestic bottlenecks, which will not only reinforce the comparative disadvantage of the

---

[9] On the notion of suction, see Kornai [62]. For a brief analysis and discussion of the literature on so-called investment cycles in planned economies and their relationship to the balance of trade, see Wolf [131].

FTOs in manufactures in terms of reliability of deliveries, but may also cause actual imports (exports) in a given plan period to be greater (less) than planned (Brown [24]).

A fourth policy objective having at least an indirect impact on foreign trade in the CPE is full employment and, indeed, individual job security. Enterprises and their employees are meant to be relatively insulated from adverse exogenous disturbances, particularly in the short- and medium term. Much of the protection of enterprises from exogenous disturbances emanating from abroad is provided by the system of price equalization. Extensive direct or "subjective" subsidization of enterprises, often by means of individually negotiated tax exemptions, credit preferences and other devices, is also used to cushion firms from the effects of unanticipated adverse shocks. A more fundamental way to cushion society from economic uncertainty, however, is to use the institutions of central planning to restrain the economy's involvement in foreign trade in the first place. This approach effectively results in a policy of widespread import substitution, and reinforces the aforementioned bias toward trade aversion that one might expect from the logic of central planning itself (see the preceding subsection).

A final characteristic of CPEs that affects foreign trade but which is difficult to pinpoint in terms of origin (i.e., system versus policy), is the phenomenon know as "storming." This refers to the feverish mobilization of resources by enterprises at the end of a plan period in order to meet planned production targets. Storming also characterizes the export experience of many CPEs, and may result in a number of adverse effects, including a loss of customer confidence in the exporter's delivery reliability, reduced product quality, and terms of trade losses as products are suddenly unloaded on world markets at the end of a plan period, regardless of current market conditions.[10]

The foregoing institutions and fundamental policies are critical in determining the foreign trade behavior of CPEs at both the microeconomic and macroeconomic levels. With these determinants and their behavioral implications in mind, the next two section will undertake, respectively, a closer examination of microeconomic

---

[10] Recent empirical evidence on storming is provided by Rostowski and Auerbach [103].

decisionmaking in foreign trade, and the relationship of foreign trade to the centrally planned macroeconomy and macroeconomic balance and adjustment in the CPE.

3. FOREIGN TRADE DECISIONMAKING

The efficiency of foreign trade and the exchange rate

In the stylized market economy, most or all foreign trade is carried out by autonomous, profit-maximizing enterprises. Decisions to export or import are made on the basis of profitability calculations in terms of prices and costs expressed in domestic currency. A difference between the domestic currency price of a product and the domestic currency equivalent of the foreign trade price (inclusive of trade tax or subsidy) will represent an opportunity for commodity arbitrage, and arbitrage will in turn eliminate the price differential. In equilibrium:

$$P_i = P_i^* e(1 + t_i), \qquad (2)$$

where P_i and P_i^*, respectively, denote the domestic currency and foreign currency price of the ith product, e is the official exchange rate, expressed as the domestic currency price of a unit of foreign exchange, and t_i is the *ad valorem* explicit or implicit trade tax or subsidy levied by the government on the ith good.

Because most or all domestic prices in the stylized ME are market-clearing, and their structure is likely to reflect at least roughly the underlying pattern of scarcities in the domestic economy, enterprise trade conducted so as to satisfy the international commodity arbitrage assumption implicit in Eq. (2) is also likely to maximize the static gains from trade potentially available to the market economy as a whole.

In the CPE, by contrast, the system of price equalization taxes and subsidies insulates, as we have seen, both the level and structure of domestic prices from world market prices. This fundamental insulation may be summarized by:

$$P_i = P_i^* e'(1 + \alpha_i), \qquad (3)$$

where P_i^* is defined as before, e' is the *valuta* (or external) exchange rate, P_i is the domestic currency price at which the ith good is transferred between a FTO and domestic industrial or wholesale organizations, and α_i represents the ex post implicit variable commodity-specific trade tax rate on the ith product.[11]

Because both the domestic price for the ith good and the valuta exchange rate are typically fixed for long periods by the authorities, α_i will vary inversely with fluctuations in the foreign currency price that is paid or received by the FTO. The quantity $(1 + \alpha_i)$ is a variable that is equal to the ratio of the domestic currency price (P_i) to the so-called *valuta* price of the product $(P_i' = P_i^* e')$. It is this latter price that is typically used by CPEs in the valuation of foreign trade in their official statistics. The variable $(1 + \alpha_i)$ may be thought of as a commodity-specific implicit internal exchange rate. Because the valuta exchange rate will usually differ between trade with MEs and trade with other CPEs, respectively, and because this difference in general only coincidentally would reflect the differences in the prices at which identical goods are sold in both types of foreign market (see Section 4), in general there will be a different implicit internal exchange rate for each commodity-regional currency combination.

Missing in the CPE are the relatively straightforward relationships between prices and opportunity costs found in the stylized market economy. Domestic producer prices, for example, are typically based in the CPE on the historical average cost of production of the relevant industrial branch. These costs will generally be distorted; for instance they may not include a capital charge. Furthermore, producer prices are held fixed for long periods and over fairly wide ranges of output. These administratively set prices therefore will not, in general, reflect changes in underlying domestic opportunity costs of production.

The basic indeterminacy of the foreign trade decision under primitive central planning is illustrated in Figure 1. In panel A is drawn an upward sloping supply curve reflecting the "real" increasing domestic marginal cost of producing an importable. For simplicity, the planners' demand for this good, indicated by D( ), is assumed to be perfectly inelastic. In panel B the *valuta* price of the

---

[11] The notation and analysis is from Wolf [132].

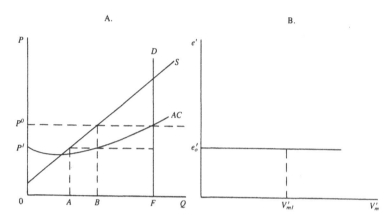

FIGURE 1   The indeterminacy of foreign trade decisions under primitive central planning.

importable $(P'_m = P^*_m e' = e'$, where P^*_m is set equal to unity) is plotted against the volume of imports of this product. Assume that last period this "small" CPE followed an autarkical policy, producing OF of the importable, and that the planners happen to have realistically estimated the real average full costs (AC) of production at OF of output. They set the domestic price accordingly at P_0. Now let the planners ponder whether they should import this period and if so, how much. They have arbitrarily set the *valuta* exchange rate equal to e'_0. Were they to ignore the arbitrariness of the exchange rate and to emulate the efficiency criteria of the market economy, they would authorize imports equal to AF ($=V'_{ml}$). But they do not know the shape of the real domestic supply curve, and in any event ideological scruples might keep them from following such a marginalist approach. Their best measure of domestic cost is P_0. Because P_0 is greater than the *valuta* cost of the importable, they might be tempted to import this good. There is nothing to tell them, however, exactly how much to import. Only if they knew the slope of the average cost curve (AC) would they be led to import a quantity (BF) that would equate average domestic cost with the *valuta* price of the import ($P_1 = e'_0$). The latter price, in any event, is an arbitrary measure of the true domestic cost, in terms of the production of exportables, of importing this product, because the valuta exchange rate has been established arbitrarily.

The planners will soon recognize that unlike the exchange rate in the ME, their official valuta exchange rate does not embody economically useful information. Only by coincidence would this exchange rate even approximate the domestic accounting cost of earning foreign exchange (i.e., it would in that case yield an average internal exchange rate $(1 + \alpha)$ of unity), let alone the real cost. As a practical matter, the valuta exchange rates of CPEs have historically understated the average domestic accounting cost of earning a unit of foreign exchange in convertible currency markets (Holzman [54]).

Relatively early in the development of centrally planned economic systems it was realized that greater efficiency in foreign trade planning would depend on both improving the measures of domestic costs and use values of products, and adjusting the valuta, or external, exchange rate so as to reflect more accurately the true cost of earning foreign exchange (see Boltho [12] and Hewett [37]). As early as the late 1950s and early 1960s, economists in the CPEs were developing various indices of "foreign trade effectiveness." The basic index can be visualized as an *official internal* exchange rate. Such a rate (e''), expressed as the ratio of units of domestic currency per unit of *valuta* (P_i/P_i'), could be established for trade as a whole, or rates could be differentiated by industrial branch or commodity groupings. In effect, the official internal exchange rate is meant roughly to bridge the gap between the average domestic price of traded goods in some reference group, and their average valuta price. This exchange rate, multiplied by the external rate (e'), would be the basis for the so-called calculative price (P_i'') for the ith product:

$$P_i'' = P_i^* e' e''(1 + t_i), \qquad (4)$$

where P_i^* and e' are as defined earlier, e'' is the relevant official internal exchange rate, and t_i is the actual explicit trade tax (subsidy) rate for the ith product. The calculative price for the ith good would be equal to its actual domestic currency price (P_i) only in the event that $e''(1 + t_i)$ were equal to the *implicit* internal exchange rate for that product; i.e., only if the product in question happened to have a ratio of its domestic to foreign currency price that was equal to the average for its reference group (compare (3) and (4)).

The calculative price is a standard against which the domestic wholesale or producer price of a product can be compared. If the calculative price for a product is greater than its domestic price, for example, this would suggest to the planners that this good would be a profitable export, at least relative to other products in its reference group. Insofar as the products constituting a particular reference group have enough in common to justify the assumption of similar distortions in their average costs of production, such an approach may be useful. It leaves basically unsolved, however, the comparision of the relative export profitability of products from different reference groups (Winiecki [121]). Moreover, because domestic prices generally will not reflect the real marginal cost of domestic production, the use of official internal exchange rates derived in this way will not provide a reliable guide to the most efficient level of trade for either individual products or for the economy as a whole.

These evident limitations of the more primitive foreign trade effectiveness indices soon led to attempts to develop shadow exchange rate measures using large-scale linear programming models (Trzeciakowski [113, 114]). The objective was to optimize some objective function (which could be to minimize costs or to maximize consumption), subject to linear constraints with respect to production possibilities and the balance of trade. Fixed coefficient production functions and constant costs were assumed, for both domestic- and foreign-produced goods. The optimization process yielded requirements for real trade flows by commodity, and it implied a domestic currency shadow price for each traded good.

The foreign trade implications of this approach are illustrated in Figure 2. Importables are arranged in descending order according to the ratio of their estimated domestic shadow price (Z_{mi}) to their *valuta* price (P'_{mi}).[12] Exportables are arranged in ascending order of their real domestic cost of production (Z_{xi}) to their valuta price (P'_{xi}). On the horizontal axis is measured the cumulative valuta value of these imports and exports. Because marginal costs are assumed to be constant for all products, the valuta expenditure ($V'_m(\ )$) and revenue ($V'_x(\ )$) curves in the figure are in fact

---

[12] The following discussion follows closely that of Wolf [132], which draws in turn mainly on Trzeciakowski [113, 114] and Shagalov [104].

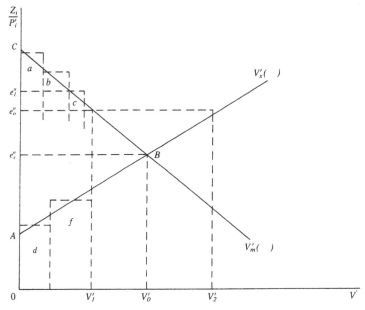

FIGURE 2   Determining the optimal exchange rate under central planning.

approximations to bar graphs composed of individual products (for example, importables a, b, and c, and exportables d and f).

Imports are viewed as profitable only if the real saving of resources they entail or their use value to the national economy is greater than the real value of the domestic resources used to earn the foreign exchange for their purchase. Trade should therefore be expanded, in the order indicated in the diagram, only as long as $(Z_{mi}/P'_{mi}) > (Z_{xi}/P'_{xi})$, where the ith products are the marginal importable and the marginal exportable, respectively. Consequently, the "optimal" value of balanced trade will be equal to V'_0, which is the valuta value of exports and imports corresponding to the intersection of the $V'_x(\ )$ and $V'_m(\ )$ curves. This intersection also yields the shadow internal exchange rate, e''_s, at which the average domestic relative shadow price of the marginal export and import is equal to their relative price in the foreign market. When trade is balanced at V'_0, the net welfare gain to the economy is measured by triangle ABC. A different pattern of trade, whether or not balanced, can be shown to yield a smaller sum of combined producer and consumer surplus in foreign trade.

Although Figure 2 looks exactly like the foreign exchange market diagram frequently constructed for the market economy, it is actually quite different. The downward sloping demand schedule for foreign exchange in the ME, for example, indicates the aggregate demand of autonomous economic agents for foreign exchange, at different exchange rates that are, from their standpoint, exogenous. In Figure 2, on the other hand, the vertical axis measures Z_i/P_i, or what may be called the *real* implicit internal exchange rate of the ith product in a CPE. Here, the $V'_m(\ )$ schedule could be visualized as reflecting planners' demand for valuta at different shadow internal exchange rates, provided they are willing to plan trade on this basis. But it is the planners themselves who will determine the applicable shadow exchange rate, depending on their trade balance target. Moreover, the slopes and positions of $V'_x(\ )$ and $V'_m(\ )$, which jointly determine the shadow exchange rate corresponding to a given trade balance target, in turn reflect the underlying preferences of the planners regarding the structure of domestic production and consumption.

It should also be noted that the foreign exchange market curves for the market economy represent the summation of interdependent foreign exchange schedules relating to individual products. This interdependence is basically missing in Figure 2. Compare, for example, the impact on import volumes of an increase in the exchange rate in a ME, with a similar change in the shadow exchange rate in a CPE. In the market economy, an increase in the exchange rate would generally lead to a reduction in imports of all products, but by amounts that varied directly with their different price elasticities of import demand. In the CPE, on the other hand, an increase in the shadow internal rate from e''_0 to, say, e''_1, would lead the planners to eliminate entirely imports of product c, but goods a and b, with real implicit internal exchange rates higher than e''_1, would presumably be imported in the same quantities as before. This basic difference reflects the underlying assumption, in this shadow price approach, of constant costs and use values for individual products.

Finally, although the "optimal" or shadow internal exchange rate in Figure 2 leads to balanced trade, it should not be confused with the notion of an "equilibrium" exchange rate in the market economy. If the planners relinquished direct control over the allocation of resources, trade, foreign exchange and international capital flows, there would be no reason to expect that the market forces let loose would lead to a market-clearing, or equilibrium, exchange rate equal to e_s'' in the figure.

In some CPEs, the nominal foreign trade profit (T) earned by the FTOs (see Eq. (1)) is used as a measure of both the "budgetary effectiveness" of foreign trade (i.e., T indicates the net price equalization levies on foreign trade accruing to the budget—see Section 4)), and the gains from international trade. It can be shown, however, that T is a good approximate measure of the economy's static gain from foreign trade only if (1) the domestic price structure reflects real relative scarcities (in other words, each of the P_i equal the respective Z_i), *and* (2) valuta trade is balanced and/or the official valuta exchange rate is equal to the shadow valuta exchange rate. Otherwise, T may provide a misleading measure of trade gains, and in any event it will provide no information about whether the level or composition of trade is at or near the optimum, from the standpoint of economic efficiency.[13]

Even in those CPEs in which the shadow pricing approach has been accepted, at least in principle, as an improved guide to determining the volume and pattern of foreign trade, there are still debates about what is the proper basis for determining the shadow prices to be used. Some economists argue for shadow prices based on a linear optimization model, as above; others suggest that such an approach is impractical and that estimates of "full" costs of production, namely, those that add to domestic accounting prices an imputed capital charge, would be sufficient.[14] Indeed, there are a number of practical problems associated with the estimation of

---

[13] Wolf [132]. It should also be noted that while the overall static gain from foreign trade will indeed be approximated by T when valuta trade is balanced, even in the event of a discrepancy between the shadow and official valuta exchange rates, the nominal profit earned on exports will nevertheless understate (overstate) the static gain on exports, and the nominal profit on imports will overstate (understate) the static gain on imports, to the extent that the official exchange rate is below (exceeds) the shadow exchange rate. A detailed discussion of measures of the budgetary effectiveness of foreign trade appears in Gardner [35].

[14] Gardner [35] dicusses this issue in respect of the Soviet Union; also see Shagalov [105].

meaningful shadow prices in a growing economy that in general is not characterized by market-clearing prices (Zakharov and Shagalov [139]).

Even if agreement is possible with respect to how best to estimate domestic internal shadow prices, what is in part an ideological aversion to marginalism may still lead to a reluctance in the CPE to setting the official internal exchange rate equal to the "shadow" rate estimated along the lines of Figure 2. Two alternatives that have been proposed would set the official internal exchange rate equal to the *weighted average* shadow rate for the previous period's exports, or imports, respectively. Assume, for simplicity, that *valuta* trade last period was balanced at OV_0' in Figure 2. The weighted average shadow rate for last period's exports would lie somewhere between A and e_s'' on the vertical axis. Clearly, many exports with a higher shadow rate (up to e_s'') would also be profitable. Setting the internal rate below e_s'' would lead to a trade deficit. Fixing the internal rate equal to the average import rate for the preceding period (which would fall between C and e_s'') would constitute an improvement over the previous approach, for it at least would be taking into account the economic value to the country of obtaining foreign exchange. Nevertheless, it would lead the planners to over-export, and would also be non-optimal (Gardner [35] and Shagalov [105]). It has been observed, however, that as a practical matter setting the official internal exchange rate by splitting the difference between the average export and import rates might roughly approximate the true shadow rate (Shagalov and Faermark [106]).

The CPE offer curve

Analysis of the institutions of CPE foreign trade, together with available empirical evidence, suggest that FTOs have at best quite limited autonomy with respect to the level, commodity composition and geographical pattern of their trade.[15] The effective offer curve of a CPE is therefore likely to be determined by the central planners themselves, rather than by the combined activities of

---

[15] Indirect empirical evidence on the limited autonomy of FTOs is presented in Wolf [127].

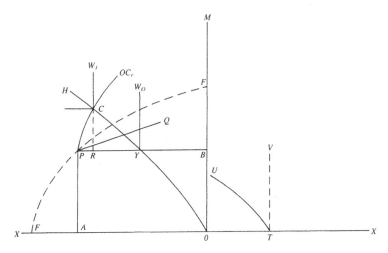

FIGURE 3   Derivation of the offer curve for the price-insensitive centrally planned economy.

mutually independent and autonomous enterprises, as in the stylized market economy.

An extreme but quite possibly realistic portrayal of the CPE would be of an economy that is fundamentally insensitive, in its domestic resource allocation decisions, to short- and medium-run changes in world market prices.[16] Planners might be considered as price-insensitive in the following respects. First, the plan for domestic output might well be rigid and unresponsive, at least for the duration of the plan period, to changes in world market conditions. Consequently, while from a purely technical standpoint the CPE may have a continuously differentiable production possibilities function (*FF* in Figure 3, which indicates the different feasible combinations of output of two composite tradables, *X* and *M*), the planners are assumed to constrain output to a fixed production point (*P*) on what amounts to production block *APB*.

Second, rather than permit the domestic availability of goods for consumption to be determined by consumers' actual rates of

---

[16] For the basic model, see Wolf [127].

commodity substitution (which, in any event, are not accurately reflected in the administratively set structure of relative prices), the planners are assumed to allocate these goods to the domestic market in predetermined proportions. Any change in the economy's real income in the short- or medium run, arising from a change in its external terms of trade or an unexpected change in domestic output, leads the planners to reallocate the two composite tradables domestically in a way that is independent of the prevailing price structure on world markets. In other words, the planners have what approximates a family of fixed-coefficient preference functions. The consumption possibilities for consumers in the CPE are therefore traced out, in the lefthand panel of Figure 3, by the income consumption path $0H$. The planners are assumed to be rational, in that they attempt to maximize their own welfare by attaining the highest possible point on $0H$, subject to a fixed domestic output mix and world market conditions.

Although the planners may be essentially price insensitive in their domestic production and consumption decisions in the short- and possibly even the medium run, they may well attempt to arrange foreign trade over longer periods in accordance with their perceptions of the economy's "fundamental comparative advantage."[17] In other words, over longer periods of time the planners' marginal propensities to (have society) consume the two tradables may change, affecting the shape of the income-consumption path $0H$ in the figure. Moreover, in response to secular terms of trade shifts and changes in imperfectly measured domestic opportunity costs, the planners will move the planned production point P along a shifting FF curve.

Placing the origin of the rest-of-world's offer curve (OC_r) at production point P, and then pivoting this curve on P, traces out an offer curve for the CPE that can be redrawn in the right-hand side panel of Figure 3 as UT. As the planners' marginal propensity to consume the exportable (importable) approaches unity, the consumption path outwards from point Y in the lefthand panel would approach a horizontal (vertical) line, and the offer curve in the right-hand side panel would approach as well a horizontal (vertical) line.

---

[17] On the notion of fundamental comparative advantage, see Rosefielde [102].

More formally, the elasticity of a trade-offer curve, assuming some constant value constraint for the export normalized balance of trade, may be expressed as:

$$\varepsilon = \beta + m - 1, \tag{5}$$

where ε is the price elasticity of export supply with respect to a change in its relative price ($\varepsilon = \hat{X}/\hat{q}$, where q is the terms of trade, and a caret denotes the percentage change in a variable), β denotes the net substitution effect in domestic demand and supply ($\beta = (S\eta_s - D\eta_d)M^{-1}$, where S and D represent domestic output and consumption, respectively, of the importable, and η_s and η_d are the elasticities of supply and of compensated demand for the importable, respectively, with respect to the relative price), and m is the marginal propensity to consume the importable.[18]

For the stylized market economy, X and M are usually assumed to be normal goods (in other words, $0 < m < 1.00$) and there is assumed to be substitution in both domestic production and consumption ($\eta_s > 0$ and $\eta_d < 0$). As long as the substitution effects are large enough, $(\beta + m)$ will exceed unity and the ME's offer curve will have a positive slope. A departure from this stylized model may be found in the "vent for surplus" theory of international trade, in which by implication a market economy's offer curve could be relatively steeply sloping or even, in the extreme case, vertical. In the extreme case, in which the economy is considered to have perfectly inelastic domestic demand for its exportable, with respect to both income and relative price, together with immobile factors of production which tend to fix its production point, β in Eq. (5) will approximate zero, m will approximate unity, and the offer curve elasticity, ε, will approximate zero.[19]

In the price-insensitive CPE, on the other hand, β will equal zero and the elasticity of the offer curve will be negative (that is, it will be backward bending) as long as the exportable is not an inferior

---

[18] This expression is derived by totally differentiating the normalized trade balance constraint $(X = q^{-1}M(1-k)^{-1}$, where k is a constant and is equal to zero when balanced trade is assumed) with respect to q, and manipulating and simplifying the resulting expression. See Wolf [127].

[19] The "vent for surplus" theory of international trade in this form has frequently been applied to various developing countries. For an elaboration of this theory see Myint [86].

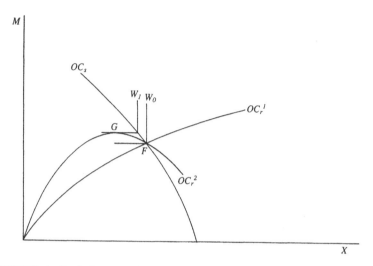

FIGURE 4 Trade between the price-insensitive centrally planned economy and market economies.

good in domestic consumption (in other words, $m < 1.00$). From Eq. (5) it is also clear, however, that if the assumption of extreme price-insensitivity is relaxed (i.e., either domestic production and/or planners' demand is price sensitive over the relevant time horizon), a positive offer curve elasticity would be possible.

In analyzing the behavioral implications of this type of CPE offer curve, it will be convenient to look separately at trade with market economies, as a group, and with other centrally planned economies. The CPE's own offer curve (OC_s) is redrawn in Figure 4, along with alternative offer curves for the composite ME that it faces. Unlike the offer curve for the price-insensitive CPE, the ME's offer curve is drawn conventionally with a positive slope (relative to the M axis, where the CPE's importable M, is the composite ME's exportable). The backward bending offer curve of the CPE implies that as its terms of trade with MEs improve (deteriorate), it will reduce (increase) its offer of exports to the market economies. In effect, because foreign trade is mainly driven by the planners' demand for imports, the planners will be preoccupied with the country's terms of trade and not, as in the case of autonomous enterprises in the market economy, with the separate prices of imports and exports, respectively.[20]

If the ME offer curve is elastic (i.e., OC_r^1) at its intersection with the CPE offer curve, the CPE's planners can maximize their welfare by trading at F. Under these conditions, and unlike the planners in a hypothetical price-sensitive CPE or policymakers in a ME who may be considering the imposition of the "optimum tariff," the planners in the price-insensitive CPE will be indifferent as to whether the FTOs as a group have external market power. In other words, the planners' trade offer will be the same regardless of whether OC_r through F is a straight line (in which case the CPE is a "small" country), or is as shown. If the ME offer curve is inelastic at F (i.e., OC_r^2), however, the CPE's planners would maximize their welfare by moving off their own offer curve to the unit elastic point on OC_r^2, at G. In this case, the CPE would behave as a revenue maximizer in foreign trade.[21].

In contrast to the market economy or the hypothetical price-sensitive CPE, each of which, if a "large" country in world trade, may decide to utilize its market power to the full by imposing the "optimum tariff," the price-insensitive CPE that faces an *elastic* ME offer curve has itself a well-defined offer schedule. This is true regardless of whether the CPE has market power. Because it has a well-defined offer curve in this sense, it will in theory be vulnerable to the exercise of market power by the composite ME it faces in world trade.[22] Empirical evidence suggests that this price-insensitive CPE model and its behavioral implications may be an appropriate

---

[20] The notion of a backward-bending offer curve in CPE foreign trade was first put forward by Brown [24] and Holzman [48], and was formalized by Wolf [127].

[21] In offer curve analysis, a country's revenue is defined as the volume of imports it can obtain by exporting. Revenue maximization involves finding that point at which marginal revenue from additional sales (exporting) is zero. Analogously to the case of demand analysis carried out with respect to nominal prices, in which marginal revenue is zero when the demand elasticity is unity, in offer curve analysis marginal revenue is zero when dM/dX is zero, in other words when $\varepsilon = 0$ for the trade partner's offer curve, which point is indicated by G in Figure 4.

[22] This model is applied to actual commercial policy issues arising in trade between CPEs and MEs by Brada [19].

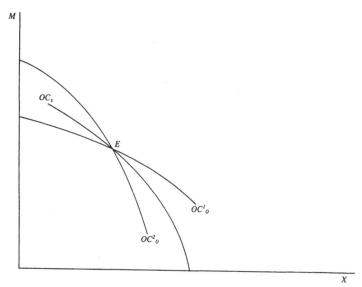

FIGURE 5   Trade between price-insensitive centrally planned economies.

stylized portrayal of at least those economies that have retained essentially the classical CPE system.[23]

In trade with other centrally planned economies, the price insensitive CPE will face a different type of situation. If other CPEs are equally price-insensitive, their composite offer curve (OC_0^1 or OC_0^2 in Figure 5) will also be backward sloping. In effect, both CPEs will face offer curves that are inelastic throughout their entire range. (Observe that the intersection of the two offer curves at E will yield a stable equilibrium in the event that the composite "other" CPE offer curve intersects OC_s from the inside (i.e., OC_0^1).) Trade would take place at E if the planners in each CPE ignored their own market power in bilateral trade. If they choose to utilize their monopoly power, however, the result is, as in most cases of

---

[23] See Wolf [127, 128]. Hewett [39], however, would argue that the trading behavior of relatively small and trade dependent CPEs may differ substantially from that of larger and less trade dependent planned economies. So-called "East–West" trade issues fall outside the scope of this essay. A short summary of the issues and literature in this area is provided by Wolf [129].

bilateral monopoly, indeterminate, and will depend *inter alia* on the relative bargaining power of the two trade partners.

The prospect of bilateral bargaining and the general lack of international commodity arbitrage in trade among CPEs suggests that considerable potential exists for price discrimination in such trade, and that such possiblities would be most favorable for that CPE which is a potentially relatively large trader. Available evidence suggests that considerable price discrimination does exist in trade among CPEs, but in practice it has been determined by several factors in addition to the relative size of the respective trading partners.[24]

The foregoing portrayal of bilateral bargaining over the terms of trade between any two CPEs is complicated by the likelihood that both partners have distorted domestic price structures. As noted earlier, each CPE's structure of domestic prices is distorted in general from both underlying domestic scarcity relations and world market relative prices. Consequently, the planners in each CPE know that in general neither domestic price structure will reflect the pattern of relative scarcities existing either internally, or within the CMEA as a whole. To rely on bilateral bargaining of prices and quantities, as portrayed in Figure 5, without reference to some regional standard, would yield a very complex process and a potential degree of price discrimination among different combinations of trade partners that could prove detrimental to attempts to develop trade and economic integration more generally among the planned economies.

One solution to this problem, and indeed the one adopted in principle very early by members of the CMEA, was to (1) strive for uniformity of pricing in intra-CMEA trade, and (2) base these prices at least indirectly on the level and structure of world market prices that characterize trade among market economies and between market economies and centrally planned economies. Under successive price-setting schemes adopted by members of the

---

[24] An early recognition of the potential for price discrimination in trade among CPEs is found in Ellis [30]. Early studies of price discrimination within the CMEA include Mendershausen [82, 83] and Holzman [45, 46]. The issue has been reopened by the controversial work of Marrese and Vanous [77]. Wolf [133] has empirically examined this issue in the case of Soviet trade with developing CPEs and developing market economies.

CMEA, documented world market prices have been adjusted for various factors, including perceived monopoly forces operating in world trade and cyclical fluctuations, and the final "contract" prices are then negotiated bilaterally on this basis. Because of this bilateral bargaining subject to CMEA "price rules," however, *de facto* price discrimination can and does still occur in trade among CPEs. Moreover, because the degree of strict documentation of world prices that is available for manufactures, which are subject to significant product differentation, is less than that for fuels, raw materials and other intermediate products, and because the degree of adjustment may vary among products, the average structure of relative prices in trade among centrally planned economies has tended to differ from that found on world markets. Specifically, the average intra-CMEA price for manufactures relative to primary products, other intermediates and food, has consistently tended to be higher than on the world market.[25]

With their mutual trade being conducted in general at relative prices different from those prevailing on world markets, significant arbitrage prospects, at least in theory, will be opened up for individual CPEs. The relative rigidity of the foreign trade planning apparatus in such economies, however, together with the possibility that they may write limitations on re-exports into their bilateral trade agreements may, in practice, constrain the amount of arbitrage that can occur.[26]

It should also be noted that inasmuch as intra-CMEA trade in general takes place at relative prices that reflect neither the partners' domestic relative scarcities nor world market prices, it is possible that a centrally planned economy, despite trading according to its "fundamental comparative advantage," could incur a net

---

[25] See Ausch [5], Marer [71] and Marrese and Vanous [77, 79]. The basis for establishment of foreign trade prices in intra-CMEA trade is reviewed in Hewett [37], Marrese and Vanous [77] and Dietz [28]. Empirical evidence on intra-CMEA pricing practices is reported in van Brabant [118]. The literature on the differences between world market and intra-CMEA foreign trade price structures, and regarding price discrimination within the CMEA, is controversial, and includes, in addition to the above: Mendershausen [82, 83], Holzman [45, 46, 57], Köves [68], Brada [20], Wolf [134] and Dietz [28, 29].

[26] On the possibilities for and limitations to arbitrage for the CMEA countries, see Marrese and Vanous [78] and Bergson [9].

welfare loss, in a narrow efficiency sense, from trade with other centrally planned economies. Two types of losses, in an opportunity cost sense, are possible. One type would be associated with transactions with other centrally planned economies at terms of trade that are inferior to those at which the CPE can trade with market economies (Marrese and Vanous [77]). The other would be associated with the CPE producing at a point on its production possibilities function at which the terms of trade is different from the marginal rate of transformation (i.e., the slope of the production possibilities frontier). In this second case, which as noted earlier is quite plausible for the CPE, particularly if it is relatively price-insensitive, it is possible but by no means necessary that it could end up with a consumption point inside its production possibilities frontier (for example, imagine a CPE producing at point P in Figure 3 and exporting X at terms of trade PQ). In other words, trade would result in a welfare position inferior to that attained under autarky. This outcome could occur in its trade with either market economies or other CPEs, or both. In practice, there would be little reason for planners to engage in trade with market economies on such a basis, but in trade with other planned economies broader objectives than simple economic efficiency *per se* might dominate. For example, one or more centrally planned economies might view the attainment of relative economic self-sufficiency among the planned economies as a group as a desideratum that warranted, for these particular CPEs, an unfavorable terms of trade.[27] Because the planners in a CPE may have such broader objectives in mind, it should not necessarily be concluded that trade patterns that suggest positive opportunity costs or, in the extreme case, even a net welfare loss *vis-à-vis* an autarkical trade position, are "irrational" from the planners' standpoint.

Other issues

The logic of central planning suggests that if left to their own devices, the planners would prefer to negotiate volumes and prices

---

[27] This is a controversial issue, on which perspective is offered by Bergson [9] and Gardner [33, 34]. Hewett [40] and McMillan [80, 81] have suggested that in the 1960s the Soviet Union had a net welfare loss, in efficiency terms, in its trade with Eastern Europe. This is disputed by Rosefielde [98, 100, 101].

of both exports and imports as a package in their dealings with other economies or groups of countries. In other words, the planners will have uppermost in mind the material balances that underpin the fulfillment of domestic plans, as well as the terms of trade, this latter factor determining the extent to which domestic production, in the form of exports, will have to be sacrificed for needed imports. In trade with market economies, the planners will be faced with the reality that most ME trade is negotiated and transacted by profit-oriented autonomous enterprises. But in trade with other centrally planned economies, the planners will be faced with a mirror image of their own institutional preferences. Consequently, trade between CPEs will not only be coordinated internally at the highest levels (as it is on the CPE side in trade with market economies), but basic trade negotiations will also take place at these levels on both sides. These negotiations will be manifested in annual and longer-term bilateral agreements (for illustrative details, see Hewett [40]).

Aside from their concern with obtaining necessary imports and with the terms of trade, CPE trade negotiators will also be interested in the balance of trade—indeed, this interest underlies their preoccupation with the terms of trade. In trade with market economies, carried out largely in convertible currencies for reasons elaborated in Section 2, the planners may want to ensure against running up persistent trade surpluses on a global basis (i.e., with MEs as a group), because exports are viewed by the planners essentially as a cost of acquiring necessary imports. They should not, in principle, be concerned with the existence or size of *bilateral* trade imbalances, however, because the convertibility of ME currencies assumes in principle the fungibility of such imbalances. A persistent global trade deficit with the MEs, however, might rationally be seen as acceptable, provided the rate of return on domestic investment facilitated by imports from MEs were perceived as higher than the real rate of interest paid on credits extended by the market economies.

Trade with other centrally planned economies, on the other hand, will come under greater pressure for strict bilateralism. The reason lies essentially in the intergovernmental negotiation of bilateral trade combined with the phenomenon of commodity inconvertibility (see Section 2). The latter suggests that the economic authorities in each CPE will be averse to accumulating trade surpluses with other individual CPEs, because the resulting financial claims, unless denominated in the convertible currencies of market economies, will not necessarily be readily convertible into commodities. Each CPE will therefore have an interest in minimizing its bilateral trade surplus with each other CPE, and even in maximizing its bilateral deficit, provided it is not required to settle the deficit with convertible currencies. The result will be a tendency towards strict bilateralism. Because each CPE's currency is inconvertible, inter-CPE trade must be carried out on the basis of either bilateral clearing agreements or, as has been the case within the CMEA since 1964, on the basis of a multilateral clearing arrangement with a clearing currency (the transferable ruble, or TR) serving as the unit of account. Even this common currency, however, must remain essentially inconvertible (and therefore this trade will be still subject to bilateralism pressures) as long as the fundamental determinant of the *de facto* inconvertibility of the national currencies, namely, commodity inconvertibility, persists. This is because each CPE knows that although the common unit of account may be, in principle, convertible into the national currencies at official exchange rates determined by the individual national governments, these currencies are not, in turn, freely convertible into commodities.[28]

Because prices in trade among CPEs are based at least indirectly on world market prices, the structure of these prices would only coincidentally clear all bilateral markets for tradables within the CMEA. In general, at the existing structure of intra-CMEA foreign trade prices (which, it will be recalled, will not in general be uniform for trade among all CPE partners), various products will be in excess demand within the CMEA and others will be in excess supply. Assume, for example, that at prevailing average intra-CMEA foreign trade prices, product M is in excess demand and X is in excess supply. In Figure 6, where stability is assumed, terms of trade tot_e would clear the CMEA market. At tot_0, which is the actual terms of trade that emerges from the combination of CMEA

---

[28] On intra-CMEA bilateralism, see van Brabant [115]. Financial payments within the CMEA are discussed by Allen [1] and Brainard [23]. Holzman [53] analyzes why the transferable ruble is not a convertible currency.

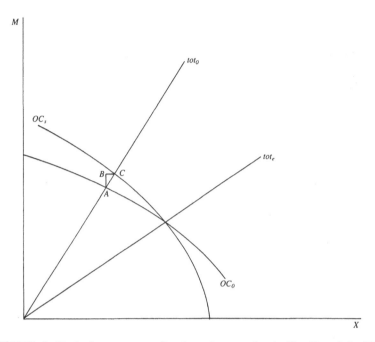

FIGURE 6   Trade between centrally planned economies in "hard" and "soft" goods.

price rules and bilateral bargaining, there is excess demand for M ($=AB$) and excess supply of X ($=BC$). What happens will depend, in principle, on the relationship between tot_0 and the relative price structure on the world market. If the relative price of X on the world market is equal to or greater than tot_0, then the CPE with offer curve OC_s would find it profitable to switch part (or all) of its exports of X to the world market in exchange for M, and eliminate the excess demand (supply) for M (of X) within the CMEA. If, on the other hand, the relative price of X on the world market is less than tot_0, this distortion might induce the "other" centrally planned economy (with offer curve OC_0) to shift some of its export offer of M to the world market, and CPE with offer curve OC_s might be induced to arbitrage, by re-exporting to the world market M purchased within the CMEA and re-exporting to the other CPE some of its imports of X from the world market. Excess demand pressures for M and excess supply pressures for X within the CMEA would in this case be exacerbated.

This second case has tended to characterize intra-CMEA trade, and the result has been the dubbing of goods in perennial excess demand within the CMEA as "hard" goods and those in excess supply, at prevailing prices, as "soft" goods. The CMEA market for the former is firm and those goods can easily be sold, without discount, for convertible currency on world markets. The opposite situation prevails for "soft" goods. Within the CMEA, fuels, food, raw materials and various semi-processed products have typically been "hard" goods, whereas finished manufactures and some semi-finished products have typically been considered as "soft" goods.

Distorted relative prices of this nature, together with inter-governmental trade negotiations and commodity inconvertibility, have led to a phenomenon in intra-CMEA trade known as "structural bilateralism." This means, in effect, that a CPE will be willing to give up so-called hard goods in export to another CPE only to the extent that it may obtain in return a bundle of hard goods of roughly equivalent aggregate value (at intra-CMEA trade prices). Soft goods, on the other hand, will be exchanged as a bundle, for an equivalent value of soft goods.[29] To the extent that one CPE agrees to supply another with hard goods with a value above and beyond reciprocal deliveries of hard goods, it may demand valuation at world market prices and settlement of the hard goods trade surplus in convertible currencies (Pécsi [92] and Fink [31]).

The logic of central planning might also suggest that the planners would want to trade more, *ceteris paribus,* with other CPEs than with market economies. To the degree that the rigidities of the centrally planned system and policies such as over-full employment planning lead to bottlenecks and significant uncertainties regarding the domestic supply of important inputs, however, the planners as a practical matter might welcome expanded trade with MEs as a type of safety valve. The ultimate geographical pattern of a CPE's trade,

---

[29] Structural bilateralism and its causes are explained in depth by van Brabant [115]. That this phenomenon has not tended to characterize Soviet trade with individual East European countries is implicit in the work of Marrese and Vanous [77, 79], and is discussed by Holzman [57].

however, will be jointly determined by a range of considerations, including natural resource and factor endowments, political factors, and economic policy objectives, as well as systemic considerations. There is evidence that mutual trade within the CMEA is much higher than it is within customs unions composed of market economies such as the European Economic Community, but it should be noted that it is very difficult to sort out quantitatively the separate impacts on trade intensity of systemic factors, political considerations, and multilateral attempts to integrate these economies.[30]

The ongoing attempts of CMEA members to integrate their economies in ways that go beyond the negotiation of bilateral trade flows, lie outside the scope of this essay. It is noteworthy, however, that various system-related factors that tend to limit the efficiency and degree of specialization of CPE trade more generally, will tend to impede to some extent the ability of the planners and the enterprises to make the type of micro-economic calculations and decisions that are necessary ingredients of transnational agreements on specialization and cooperation in production.[31] In addition, the policy objectives of preserving national sovereignty and developing a diversified economy, combined with the difficulty of accurately measuring economic costs and benefits, may lead policymakers in CPEs to follow a "limited regret" strategy with respect to integration (Neuberger [88]). In effect, they may agree to a specialization agreement with another planned economy only if the expected gains from the agreement exceed the possible losses by a sufficiently large amount, and if either the probability of a worst case outcome is very low or the possible magnitude of loss in such a case is relatively small. The result will be a tendency to specialize only in those industries, such as raw material or energy extraction, in which the output possibilities, costs, and economies to scale are relatively easy to measure. At the same time, intra-branch trade among CPEs, particularly in machinery and equipment, may be favored by the

---

[30] See Hewett [38]. Hewett [42] summarizes the empirical evidence regarding the determinants of the geographical pattern of CMEA trade. On the notion of CMEA as a "customs union," see Holzman [52, 56].

[31] Marer and Montias [75] discuss this issue in greater detail.

commodity group bargaining that occurs as the result of the above-mentioned "structural bilateralism" and the tendency of intra-CMEA negotiations on reciprocal deliveries to occur within the context of specialized commissions established for individual industrial branches (Marer and Montias [75]).

The concern with multi-year plan fulfillment and the decisive involvement of the central authorities in the planning and negotiation of foreign trade could be expected to result in a degree of stability of CPE trade somewhat greater than that of the market economies. Indeed, this is one of the rationales for the establishment of the centralized planning of foreign trade in the first place. What empirical evidence that exists, however, suggests that although intra-CMEA trade values and volumes may be more stable than those among developed market economies, CMEA trade flows with developing market economies tend to be less stable or in any event no more stable than trade between the latter and the developed market economies.[32] There is also evidence that in the 1950s and early 1960s developed ME imports from CPEs were more stable than CPE imports from developed market economies (Staller [107]). The implied relative instability of CPE imports from market economies could be partly due to the effects of various policies, such as over-full employment planning, and associated domestic bottlenecks, that more than offset the stability-inducing aspects of central planning. Evidence also exists, however, that the relative instability of CPE imports from developing market economies has diminished over time, perhaps in part because of the growth of this trade relative to CPE output (Lawson and Wiles [70], and Wolf [133]). It also appears that for at least the largest CPE, the Soviet Union, import values from developing MEs with which it has bilateral clearing agreements have been more stable than its imports from other LDCs (Wolf [133]); this suggests that bilateral clearing agreements in the case of CPE trade with developing MEs may encourage stability, although other factors may be at work here as well.

---

[32] See empirical studies by Neuberger [87], Staller [107], Lawson [69], Lawson and Wiles [70] and Wolf [133].

4. FOREIGN TRADE AND THE MACROECONOMY

System-determined statistical problems in macroeconomic analysis

Analysis of the role of foreign trade in aggregate economic activity and in the process of macroeconomic adjustment in the CPE is made more difficult by several factors that are usually of only negligible significance in the case of market economies. One complication is that the official *valuta* exchange rate, at which all foreign trade is valued in national statistics, has little economic meaning in terms of purchasing power parity, clearing the market for foreign exchange, or as a price incentive for enterprises engaged in foreign trade. A second complication arises because the system of price equalization effectively insulates the domestic price level and price structure from price changes in external trade. Third, neither the domestic price level nor the price structure are in general market-clearing, and the structure of prices is generally distorted from the standpoint of economic efficiency in the Pareto-optimal sense.

These features of the CPE present several problems for the macro-economist, and also for the comparativist interested in cross-system analysis of various economic aggregates. One such issue involves the attribution of national income by sector of origin. The usual textbook definition of national income is, of course:

$$Y = A + B_T, \tag{6}$$

where Y is income, A is domestic absorption, and B_T is the trade balance expressed, as are Y and A as well, in domestic prices. As a practical matter most countries' GDP (Y') is defined, on the basis of the System of National Accounts, as the sum of national income and net indirect taxes (T), where for simplicity T will be assumed here to consist solely of net import duties and net export taxes:

$$Y' = Y + T. \tag{7}$$

Net foreign trade taxes (T) are equal to the difference between (1) the trade balance evaluated in foreign trade prices multiplied by the official exchange rate, B'_T, and (2) the trade balance evaluated in domestic market prices, B_T (Wolf [130]):

$$T = B'_T - B_T. \tag{8}$$

In the stylized market economy, T will typically be quite small relative to GDP, and most trade taxes will be determined by fixed *ad valorem* rates. In the CPE, on the other hand, the system of price equalization and the associated likely greater degree of price distortion means that implicit net trade taxes could be much larger relative to GDP than are total net trade taxes in the market economy. Their importance will be greater, the larger the disparity in the degree of price distortion between exports and imports respectively (i.e., the greater the difference between the average implicit internal exchange rates for exports and imports—see Eq. (3) and Wolf [124]).

The contribution to income of the "foreign trade sector," if it is defined inclusive of net FTO profits on price discrepancies (which, by comparison of equations (1) and (8), is seen to be equal to T), may therefore be quite different as between the CPE and the otherwise comparable ME. Likewise, if a given disturbance affects foreign trade prices, the share of the recorded change in nominal GDP that is attributed to the foreign trade sector is likely to be greater for the CPE than for the market economy, because for the latter much of the price effect will show up as changes in the nominal value of domestic output. Moreover, the existence of the price equalization system raises questions about how nominal value-added so attributed to the foreign sector in the CPE should be deflated, in moving from nominal to real measures of GDP.[33]

Another issue concerns the measurement of the trade participation ratio or degree of openness of an economy, conventionally quantified as the ratio of its exports, imports or total trade turnover to GDP or national income. This measure, used in macroeconomic modelling and policy analysis, is usually quite straightforward for market economies (although possibly not for many developing MEs), because distortions between domestic and foreign prices are generally minor, and thus the ratio of trade to income is considered to be roughly indicative of the true degree of importance of foreign trade to the national economy.

In the CPE, on the other hand, foreign trade is valued in official

---

[33] Wolf [135] and Nove [91]. The variable T may be defined a little differently from equation (8) for some CPEs, which raises additional problems of comparability. See Holzman [50] and Wolf [130].

statistics in terms of valuta prices $(V' = V'_x + V'_m = P^*_x e' Q_x + P^*_m e' Q_m)$—see Eq. (1)), whereas GDP is evaluated at domestic market prices, and both the level and the structure of the two, as earlier discussed, may be very different.[34] If the valuta exchange rate had any relationship to purchasing power parity, it could be used to convert income in domestic prices into foreign currency prices, for purposes of a comparison with the foreign currency value of a CPE's trade; but, for reasons discussed earlier, the valuta rate will typically not have any definite relationship to purchasing power parity. In this connection it should also be noted that the un-availability of an economically meaningful exchange rate also limits severely the extent to which international comparisons of income can be made that include CPEs.[35]

A third issue regards the measurement of the foreign trade magnitudes of a CPE in the first place. The main problem involves the aggregation of trade flows conducted with the market economies and with other CPEs, respectively. Trade flows with other members of the CMEA are for the most part settled in TRs, but their prices are indirectly based, as we have seen, on world market prices. For a given bundle of goods traded within the CMEA by a member country, its weighted average TR price is equal to its weighted average world market price in some convertible currency measure (say, the U.S. dollar), multiplied by some implicit price distortion parameter (which is actually a variable determined in part by the CMEA price rules and partly through bilateral negotiation), and multiplied again by the agreed-upon official CMEA TR/dollar exchange rate.[36] TR-settled trade is then converted into national trade statistics using the country's official exchange rate for the TR, which for most classical CPEs is their valuta rate. Trade settled in

---

[34] Controversial evidence on the relationship between *valuta* and domestic prices in Soviet foreign trade is provided by Treml and Kostinsky [112] and Treml [111]. The problem faced when attempting to measure the foreign trade participation ratio of a CPE is essentially the same as that involved with meaningfully relating a CPE's external debt, which will mainly be denominated in foreign currencies, to its level of income.

[35] The problems associated with the conversion of CPE income from national currency units into a measure expressed in a foreign currency are comprehensively explored in Marer [73].

[36] This exchange rate is set by the International Bank for Economic Cooperation (IBEC), an institution of the CMEA. See van Brabant [118].

convertible currencies, which is presumably carried out at or near world market prices, is on the other hand converted directly into national trade statistics using the applicable national official valuta rate.

The resulting magnitudes for TR-settled and convertible trade in the CPE's statistics will in general be non-comparable, for two reasons. First, intra-CMEA foreign trade prices are in general distorted *vis-à-vis* world market (and CPE-ME trade) prices; second, the CMEA TR/dollar rate may differ from the implicit TR/dollar cross valuta rate of each CPE. Furthermore, if all of a CPE's trade flows are converted into a common currency such as the dollar, the degree of non-comparability between TR-settled and convertible trade flows, and hence the degree of bias in the estimate of the economy's total trade, will in general differ depending on whether the TR-settled flows denominated in valuta are converted "backwards" into dollars using the country's valuta ruble exchange rate and the CMEA TR/dollar rate, or "forwards" using the national valuta dollar rate. In the first case the degree of bias in the dollar value of the TR-settled trade will be to equal to α, which is the percentage by which intra-CMEA foreign trade prices differ (when converted "backwards" into dollars) from the prices of comparable goods trading on the world market. In the second, or "forwards" conversion case, the percentage conversion bias (b) will equal:

$$b = [(1 + \alpha)e_i]/e_c - 1, \qquad (9)$$

where e_i is the CMEA-set TR/dollar rate and e_c is the national TR/dollar cross rate (Wolf [136]).

Internal and external balance

Notwithstanding these statistical issues, analysis of the CPE macro-economy can proceed using the same basic framework employed for market economies. As shown by Eqs (6)–(8), the fundamental identities relating the output and expenditure sides of national income are the same for a CPE as for a ME. Moreover, the familiar monetary definition of the balance of payments also applies:

$$B'_T = (\Delta M - \Delta D) = \Delta \text{NFA}, \qquad (10)$$

where B'_T in this case is the valuta trade balance, ΔM denotes the change in the nominal money supply (currency and deposits held by enterprises and households), ΔD is the change in *net* domestic credit extended by the CPE's banking system (i.e., gross domestic credit less the deposits of the government), and ΔNFA is the change in net foreign assets held by the CPE. (It is assumed for simplicity that the only international capital flows are associated with real trade flows.)[37]

In analysis of the stylized market economy, it is usually assumed that holders of money will be able rapidly to adjust to any temporary disequilibrium in the domestic money market. Therefore the change in the money supply in Eq. (10) is assumed to be equal to the change in the flow demand for money on the part of enterprises and households. In the CPE, on the other hand, the rigidity of domestic prices and the lack of short-term supply response by enterprises to market imbalances, particularly in the consumption goods sector, means that money holders may not always be in flow equilibrium. Changes in the money supply held by households (ΔM_h) will in general be equal to:

$$\Delta M_h = \Delta M_h^* + C^d - C, \tag{11}$$

where ΔM_h^* is the flow household demand for money, C^d is the aggregate demand for consumption goods, and C represents actual nominal consumption spending. It is not necessary to assume the existence of excess demand for consumption goods at the aggregate level (a controversial assumption) to have a build-up in excess household liquidity.[38] Microlevel imbalances, in which the accumulation of excess household liquidity is exactly offset by an

---

[37] On the balance sheet of the banking system gross assets (gross domestic credit plus gross holdings of foreign assets) equal gross liabilities (the domestic money supply plus government deposits and gross foreign liabilities). Netting out government deposits from gross domestic credit, and foreign liabilities from foreign assets, gives net domestic credit (D) plus net foreign assets (NFA) equal to the domestic money supply. For more detail, including the role of net price equalization taxes, see Wolf [124].

[38] On the controversy over the issue of chronic excess demand for consumption goods in planned economies, see Portes [95]. To the extent that households respond to excess demand for consumption goods offered by the socialized sector by bidding up prices in the "second" economy, substituting less desirable goods in abundant supply for those subject to shortage, and reducing their effective supply of labor offered to the socialized sector, they may achieve a kind of "constrained equilibrium" and may not, technically speaking, continue to possess excess liquidity. See Wolf [131], and the references therein.

increase in unplanned enterprise inventories of consumption goods, would yield in principle the same result.[39]

For the CPE, the familiar identity (10) may be written as:

$$B'_T = (\Delta M_h^* + C^d - C) - \Delta D'', \tag{12}$$

where $\Delta D''$ denotes the change in *net* domestic credit extended to government and enterprises (i.e., the change in gross credit minus the increase in their deposits), plus the change in *gross* credit extended to households (Wolf [131]). The important implication for macroeconomic stabilization in CPEs is that a particular change in net domestic credit may affect the trade balance and/or possibly the flow demand for money (in other words, by affecting velocity), as in the market economy, but also, depending upon the reaction of enterprises and the outcome of their bargaining with the authorities over access to resources, it may affect the degree of imbalance $(C^d - C)$ in the market for consumption goods. In practice, of course, net domestic credit in the CPE is to be viewed as a more or less passive variable, which reflects the accommodation by the banking system of whatever credit demands arise from enterprises in the course of attempting to implement the physical plan.

Although the price equalization system may, if the authorities desire, insulate the level and structure of domestic prices from changes in foreign trade prices, the operation of this mechanism alone does not, as is sometimes believed, necessarily insulate the domestic economy as a whole from such changes. In particular, if at full employment output the authorities were to react to, say, a deterioration in the external terms of trade by changing real trade flows—for instance, by increasing real exports and reducing real imports; that is, sliding down to the right on the backward bending offer curve of Figures 4 through 6—the domestic money supply would initially increase, exactly offsetting the decline in domestic nominal absorption. Such an increase in the money supply in this case could only be offset by the authorities by means of contractionary fiscal measures (some combination of increased taxes and/or reduced subsidies), or outright confiscation of money holdings (as in a currency reform).

The extreme cases of short-term adjustment to such a disturbance can be illustrated quite simply using Eq. (13), which is derived from

---

[39] For a more detailed discussion, including the role of inventories, see Wolf [131].

expressions (8) and (10):

$$\Delta M = (B'_T + \Delta D) = (B_T + T + \Delta D). \qquad (13)$$

In both cases it will be assumed, for simplicity, that trade initially is balanced in both valuta and domestic currency prices (in other words, T in Eq. (8) is zero). If the authorities were willing to permit the economy's net foreign assets (or reserves, loosely speaking) to fall by the amount of deterioration in the valuta balance brought on by the terms of trade deterioration, and they left real trade flows unchanged $B_T = 0$, net FTO profits (which are equal to net price equalization taxes collected by the budget, or T) would decline by an amount equal to the deterioration in the valuta trade balance $(B'_T < 0)$, and *net* domestic credit extended to the government would rise by an equal amount $(\Delta D > 0)$, reflecting the fall in budgetary revenue.[40] The domestic money supply, therefore, would remain unchanged $(\Delta M = \Delta B'_T + \Delta D = 0)$. In this case the domestic economy would remain completely unaffected by the external disturbance, although only at the expense of a decline in its net international reserves. If, at the other extreme, trade flows were manipulated by the authorities so as to maintain the initial level of the trade balance $(B'_T = 0)$, the domestic money supply would increase by the amount by which the trade balance in domestic prices improved $(\Delta M = B_T > 0)$ due to the fall in domestic absorption, while at the same time the fall in net price equalization taxes would be just offset by increased net credit to the government $(\Delta T = (-\Delta D))$ (Wolf [124]).

The *ceteris paribus* response to an exogenous adverse real disturbance in foreign trade that we might actually expect from a CPE would typically be different from that encountered in market economies. In the ME with international commodity arbitrage, an

---

[40] Observe that this does not necessarily mean that the government would now be running a budget deficit, but simply that its net surplus would be smaller than otherwise. Moreover, note that an increase in net domestic credit extended to government is a flow concept; it says nothing about the relative size of the stock of gross domestic credit extended to the government and the latter's deposits with the banking system.

exogenous deterioration in the terms of trade will lead to an immediate fall in real incomes and a shift in domestic relative prices in favor of production of the importable and consumption of the exportable. Under a fixed exchange rate regime, a temporary deterioration in the trade balance resulting from the terms of trade disturbance, and attendant decline in the real money supply (monetary policy is assumed not be accommodative), together with the loss in real income, will lead to a lower level of domestic real expenditure and eventual elimination of the trade deficit. If the ME has a flexible exchange rate, the excess demand for foreign exchange occasioned by the incipient deterioration in the trade balance will cause the ME's currency to depreciate. This will cause an increase in the domestic price level and thus a decline in the real wage and real money balances, which will in turn lead to a decline in domestic real absorption. Together with the substitution effects in domestic production and consumption engendered by the terms of trade shift, this fall in real expenditure will eliminate the excess demand for foreign exchange.

The expected reaction of the CPE with a binding trade balance constraint, as indicated earlier, would be a cutback in domestic expenditure that is essentially mandated by authorities who issue directives to the FTOs and producing enterprises to divert exportables toward foreign markets and to the FTOs to cut back on imports. Although the expenditure-reducing and trade balance outcomes are similar, in the aggregate, to those expected in the market economy, these outcomes are not obtained in the CPE as the result of economic agents responding to domestic price signals. Indeed, in the CPE, most or all short-run adjustments are quantity adjustments; with relatively rigid prices, market imbalances therefore will typically develop, particularly in the household sector but probably also to some degree in the enterprise sector. Whereas the adverse foreign trade disturbance may have a deflationary effect and an adverse impact on employment and output in the ME, particularly if money wages are sticky and the exchange rate is fixed, the impact in the CPE is more likely to be inflationary, in the sense that the buildup in excess liquidity will lead to repressed inflation on domestic markets (Holzman [48], Wiles [120] and Wolf [131]). These pressures may well be exacerbated by multiplier effects, which may be particularly severe in CPEs due to their heavy concentration of imports in intermediate products and capital goods deemed critical to domestic plan fulfillment.[41]

The almost exclusive reliance by CPE authorities on quantity adjustment, in the short run and even the medium run, also characterizes their reaction to adverse disturbances originating in the domestic economy. If again they are subject to a tight trade balance constraint, their likely reaction to, say, an adverse supply shock will be (unless initial consumption is viewed as being at the minimum tolerable level) to divert available resources to priority sectors, resulting in a buildup in excess demand pressures in other sectors such as the market for consumption goods. Likewise, the development of excess demand pressures from the demand side, a frequent occurrence in CPEs associated with so-called investment cycles, can generally be expected to result in the short- and possibly the medium run in a diversion of resources into investment and away from exports and the consumption goods market.[42] Because of the high likelihood of disequilibrium in one or more markets of the CPE in such circumstances, macro-modelling of these economies has increasingly turned toward explicitly disequilibrium approaches.[43]

Unlike their counterparts in the market economy, the authorities in the CPE are unlikely to attempt to use the exchange rate as an instrument for macroeconomic stabilization. It will be recalled from Section 2 that the net nominal profits (T) of the FTOs are typically taxed away by the budget. Although increases in these profits do not, therefore, accrue to the FTOs, it is of course possible that FTO management might still have an interest in such profits if they are indeed rewarded in part on the basis of their "budgetary effectiveness" (in other words, T; see Sections 2 and 3). Specifically, if nominal profits from exporting were positive, at the existing

---

[41] See, in particular, Wiles [120] and Holzman [51]. The various multiplier effects are elaborated in terms of a formal model by Brada [18].

[42] For a brief survey of the literature on investment cycles and their impact on external and internal balance in the CPE, see Wolf [131]; also see the references therein.

[43] For an elaborate model of internal-external balance in the CPE, in an explicitly disequilibrium framework, see Portes [94]. Also see the discussions of the work of Portes in Holzman [55] and Wolf [131]. Portes [95] surveys the literature on the application of disequilibrium econometrics to CPEs.

valuta exchange rate, the FTOs might want to maximize their export profits by manipulating export volume in such a way that the marginal revenue from exporting equaled the fixed wholesale price paid to domestic suppliers of the exportable. An increase in the valuta export price, either as the result of a rise in world market prices or of the valuta exchange rate itself, would increase (decrease) their net nominal profits (loss) on exports, and would presumably stimulate their interest in exporting. (In other words, the FTO would perceive an outward shift in the demand curve for its exports, relative to their valuta prices, and a corresponding outward (or upward, if a price taker) shift in its marginal revenue curve.) What little systematic empirical evidence that exists, however, suggests that FTOs in centrally planned economies do not respond to higher valuta export prices (*ceteris paribus*) by stepping up their exports. This suggests that either the FTOs have little interest in maximizing their "profits" (hence they are in fact only "nominal"), and/or the FTOs simply have little or no influence over the real trade flows that, along with valuta prices, jointly determine these profits.[44] Because of this lack of autonomy and/or profit "interestedness" of the FTOs, and because domestic prices in the CPE are invariant to changes in the valuta exchange rate, this exchange rate is likely to have mainly an accounting, rather than an economic, function. Moreover, a change in this exchange rate will affect the size of the valuta trade balance and the value of net price equalization taxes collected by the budget only if *valuta* trade is initially unbalanced.[45]

---

[44] Empirical evidence for the Soviet Union is provided by Wolf [127]. Gardner [35], on the other hand, presents some evidence of a positive correlation between export volumes and a measure of "budgetary effectiveness" (P'_x/P_x), but it is based on single-equation estimates that do not take into account the balance of trade constraint nor the influence of domestic activity variables.

[45] It is assumed that in the CPE, real trade flows are invariant to changes in the valuta exchange rate; for this reason, foreign currency prices for its traded goods are also invariant with respect to such changes. Consequently, the only effect of an exchange rate change is a change in valuta prices. If valuta trade (and therefore trade in foreign currency prices) is initially balanced, a change in the valuta exchange rate will not affect the valuta trade balance (in other words, $B'_T = (V^*_x - V^*_m)e'$ and $dB'_T = (V^*_x - V^*_m)\,de'$, where $V^*_x = V^*_m$). See Eq. (1) and Pryor [96] and Wolf [124].

5. ECONOMIC REFORM AND FOREIGN TRADE

Centrally planned foreign trade is arguably one of the more successful facets of central planning in practice. The state monopoly over foreign trade, together with other features of foreign trade in the CPE, has generally performed well in insulating centrally planned economies somewhat from external disturbances, and in ensuring the import of those foreign-produced goods essential to domestic plan fulfillment. On the other hand, as noted in Sections 2 and 3, many of the rigidities and inefficiencies that characterize foreign trade in the centrally planned economy are direct manifestations of more general institutional and, in some cases, policy features of the CPE. In one sense, central planning is a victim of its own success. As rapid economic development has taken place as the result of the centrally directed mobilization of resources, both the scope for further rapid growth based on such an *extensive* strategy (relying mainly on rapid accumulation of productive factors), and the capacity of the vast planning apparatus to direct the increasingly complex economy, have declined.

As early as the mid-1950s, various types of economic reform were being considered in some CPEs. Fairly limited types of reform in foreign trade, such as the experimentation with various types of "foreign trade effectiveness" indicators, and shadow exchange rates, have already been discussed in Section 3. At the same time that increased attention was being directed in these ways to raising efficiency, and more generally to the necessity for shifting from an extensive to a more *intensive* development strategy (one emphasizing the quality and efficiency of use of inputs and outputs, rather than mainly their quantity), some CPEs found their foreign trade itself to be a source of pressure for economic reform.

One hypothesis is that those CPEs that are relatively poorly endowed in natural resources, and therefore for which the potential for export of conventional "hard" goods is smaller, will be under particular pressure, as economic development proceeds, to pursue economic reform. Such economies, it is argued, will feel this pressure partly from CPE trade partners possessed with a larger hard good export potential. These partners, with which there is a tendency toward bilateralism and even "structural bilateralism" (Section 3), will push for a broader hardening of the CPE's export offer. The alternative, for the CPE that requires growing quantities of imported intermediates and high-quality capital goods for economic growth, would be to divert more of its manufactures exports toward ME markets. In either case, however, success for the relatively resource-poor CPE depends on its overcoming many of the institutional and policy constraints of the classical planned economy that tend to soften its export offers. By improving the saleability of its exportables to ME markets, the CPE would enhance its convertible currency earning capacity, which would permit increased imports of world-level capital goods and technology that in turn would foster more rapid economic growth as well as a more competitive position in all markets (Brown and Marer [25]).

Institutional arrangements of the modified planned economy

Although there are innumerable reform models, the basic choice for a CPE is between a reform that attempts to improve the efficiency of operation and the results of central planning, and one that is meant to make enterprises considerably more autonomous and to increase significantly the role of the market in the allocation of resources.[46] Insofar as foreign trade is concerned, the two basic approaches have very different implications for its organization and implementation. In the less ambitious model, which is often characterized as "perfecting" the system of planning and management, the authorities will attempt to increase the extent of coordination between FTOs and domestic enterprises or combines, perhaps subordinating the former, to some degree, to the latter.[47] More emphasis will be given to the "realized sales" or possibly valued added or profit of the industrial enterprises, as an evaluative criterion, and less to the traditional dominant criterion of gross output. Prices may play an enhanced role in resource allocation, but the prices actually prevailing in domestic transactions will continue to be almost exclusively set by the authorities. A valuta exchange

---

[46] For comprehensive taxonomies of reform approaches in planned economies, see Bornstein [13, 14].

[47] This was the approach of the German Democratic Republic in the late 1970s and early 1980s—see Wolf [132] and the references therein.

rate and a system of official internal rates will continue to characterize the foreign trade system.[48]

The economy that adopts the more far-reaching and market-oriented reform strategy will be referred to here as the "modified planned economy" (MPE).[49] The MPE has the following features that are of some relevance to foreign trade. First, detailed plans regarding enterprise inputs and outputs will no longer be developed in such close consultation with the central authorities, and these plans will in any event no longer be mandatory. Second, enterprise profits will supplant plan fulfillment as the main evaluative criterion for enterprise management. Third, enterprises will be encouraged to deal mainly "horizontally," or directly, with other firms through the market. Fourth, and in line with the expanded role for the market, greater price flexibility will be permitted for a broad range of producer and consumer goods. Fifth, enterprises will be given more autonomy with regard to wages, with assignment of the wage bill from the center being replaced by wage determination at the enterprise level, subject to various centrally decided parameters or taxes on "excessive" wage growth.

Sixth, bank credits and enterprise self-financing will become much more important in the financing of investment. Banks will be expected to use interest rates as a more significant credit-rationing device than in the CPE, and there may be some movement toward breaching the dichotomy of the enterprise and household money supplies characteristic of the classical planned economy. Seventh, the greater tolerance for market-determined prices and more decentralized wage determination, combined with the perception that consumption goods availability is a key determinant of the incentive to work, may lead the authorities in the modified planned economy to lay more stress than their CPE counterparts on the attainment of market balance and the elimination of repressed inflation.

More direct, export-oriented linkages will also be encouraged

---

[48] Gardner [35] summarizes developments along these lines in the Soviet Union in the late 1970s.

[49] For more on the basic features of a stylized MPE, see Wolf [131]. A detailed study of the prototypical MPE, Hungary, is found in Marer [74].

between domestic producers and foreign markets, with many producers being granted direct foreign trade rights or at least the ability to contract with an FTO on a strictly commission basis. This growing emphasis on direct contact between domestic producers and their export markets, which is characteristic of the reformed CPE but even more so of the MPE, could be seen as somewhat analogous to the organizational evolution, within the large corporation in market economies, from a separate *international* division, with responsibility for all of the company's foreign trade, to *world product* divisions. Each of the latter produces a separate category of products and maintains its own foreign trade apparatus, thereby achieving, in principle, a more intimate knowledge than would an international division of the corporation's markets and their changing requirements (Brada and Jackson [21]).

Finally, organic linkages will be established in the modified planned economy between domestic and foreign currency prices for an important subset of tradables. In effect, the scope of the price equalization system will be significantly reduced. The *valuta* exchange rate in any event will be replaced by a "full" exchange rate equal to, say, $e'e''$ in Eq. (4), which is commonly referred to as a *foreign trade multiplier* or *commercial* exchange rate. In the MPE the so-called calculative price for the ith product (P_i'' from Eq. (4)) becomes a regulated "transactional" price. (This price may be regulated, rather than being determined freely by the enterprises, because the domestic economy will typically be subject to considerable monopolization as the result of the agglomerations that took place under central planning, and because continuing domestic price distortions and possibly excess demand pressures will lead the authorities to restrict imports, and thereby limit foreign competition on the domestic market.) The exporting enterprise, whether an FTO or a producer with direct foreign trade rights, will now actually receive P_i'' units of domestic currency for each unit of the ith product sold abroad. Unlike the FTOs of the classical CPE, for which valuta earnings have no purchasing power, the exporting enterprise in the MPE will actually convert its foreign exchange earnings (at the new official foreign trade multiplier or commercial exchange rate) into a domestic currency that can be used on internal markets. The transaction price paid or received in foreign trade transactions is also designed to affect, either directly or indirectly, the price at which a given traded good changes hands domestically.[50]

Foreign trade decisionmaking in the MPE

Because of its hybrid character, the modified planned economy is much more difficult to "stylize" than either the CPE or the market economy. The MPE operates partly on market principles, and in part through informal mechanisms that *de facto* perpetuate many of the patterns of hierarchical bargaining and extensive bureaucratic interference in the macroeconomic decisionmaking of firms that characterize the classical centrally planned economy (Bauer [8] and Kornai [66]).

Insofar as foreign trade decisionmaking is concerned, enterprises are in principle supposed to act analogously to the profit-maximizing firm in the market economy. In reality, although their interest in after-tax profitability may not be significantly less than that of the ME firm, enterprises in the MPE may find that their after-tax profits more often than not can and will be decisively affected by their bargaining with the authorities over prices, subsidies, tax exemptions, and other special preferences. The result is that their interest in pre-tax profits may be seriously blunted— much more attention may be given to bargaining with the fiscal and credit authorities, or perhaps with the State Price Office, than to attempts to increase efficiency or to develop new export markets. Those enterprises that do earn exceptional profits, either by virtue of more efficient operations or as the result of windfall gains from taking advantage of price distortions in the foreign trade sector, may find themselves subjected to confiscatory taxation, which is designed to provide the budget with the revenues needed to subsidize other, less fortunate, enterprises. Such fiscal redistribution may well discourage the more profitable firms from seeking out new and higher-profitability export opportunities in subsequent periods (Tardos [110] and Kornai [66]).

As a practical matter the authorities may be as obsessed with

---

[50] On the transaction price system as it has evolved in Hungary since 1968, see Marer [74] and Wolf [132]. On the notion of transaction pricing in Poland, see Plowiec [93].

after-tax profitability as the enterprises themselves. An implicit goal inherited from the CPE, despite the intention to improve the efficiency of the economy through economic reforms, may be to perpetuate the life and at least the apparent viability of individual enterprises in the socialized sector. This goal is quite rational, given the even more fundamental objective, with clear antecedents in the CPE, of preserving individual job security, at both the worker and to some extent the managerial level. Moreover, local political authorities and individual segments of the governmental bureaucracy itself (such as the industrial ministries), have a vested interest in the survival of enterprises within their venue. This interest gives enterprise managers considerable leverage with the authorities regarding favorable and discretionary fiscal and credit treatment. At the same time, those with ultimate power regarding the after-tax profitability of enterprises—the governmental bureaucracy and the political authorities—will have an obvious interest in informally influencing the product mix, scale of operations, and pricing and marketing policy of the enterprises (Kornai [66]). Consequently, while in theory foreign trade decisionmaking in the MPE may be the province of profit-oriented enterprises, possessing both the formal autonomy and the responsibility to respond chiefly to market forces, in reality their decisions will be influenced to a considerable degree by various institutions, policies, practices and relationships developed over a number of years in the centrally planned economy from which the MPE has evolved.

Because of this pervasive bureaucratic intervention and the effectively "soft budget constraint" of the enterprises (Kornai [63]), and the immobility, relative to the market economy, of both labor and capital, the so-called trade elasticities of export supply and import demand (at least at the enterprise level) are likely to be lower in the MPE than in an otherwise comparable market economy.[51] But despite the continuing *de facto* similarities between the modified planned economy and the CPE, and the blunted pretax profit motive of enterprises in the MPE, if factors are more mobile than in the centrally planned economy and enterprises are at least slightly sensitive to price changes, the aggregate offer curve of

---

[51] Tardos [110] emphasizes the importance of the limitations on labor and capital mobility in the MPE.

the MPE might well have the positive slope assumed for the market economy, rather than the backward-bending shape that may characterize the CPE. This offer curve will probably be more steeply sloped, however, than that of the market economy.

Trade relations with other planned economies may be particularly complex for the MPE. Indeed, the continuing commitment to engage, say, one-half of its trade with other planned economies may constrain its own reform efforts in foreign trade, at least insofar as most of these partners remain CPEs. Many enterprises in the MPE may trade with both CPEs and market economies, and the former part of their trade may well remain subject to negotiation and even direction, at least in terms of broad aggregates, by the central authorities. In general this would tend to constrain the speed and the extent to which an MPE enterprise could respond to changing world market conditions, either by changing its product mix or diverting trade from one area to another.

Although the MPE's offer curve in trade with market economies might be positively sloped, continued central direction of trade with other planned economies could cause its offer curve *vis-à-vis* these partners to be negatively sloped. In other words, the authorities in the modified planned economy might only be interested in maintaining some minimum level of imports from other planned economies. This, combined with the continuing commodity inconvertibility of these countries' currencies (see Section 2), might lead the authorities in a MPE to enforce a contraction in export volumes offered by MPE enterprises to CPEs, in the event of an exogenous improvement in the terms of trade. If its offer curves with the two regions were as portrayed, and if an exogenous disturbance were similar in both trading areas, adjustment by the MPE might be facilitated. For instance, consider an exogenous improvement in the MPE's terms of trade with both MEs and CPEs. It could easily meet expanded demand for its exportable in the market economies by reducing its offer to its CPE partners (see Figure 6). If the disturbance were to move in opposite directions in the two areas, however, the outcome would be less clear. For example, if the MPE's terms of trade with the CPEs were to deteriorate, while they improved with the rest of the world, the MPE would want to expand exports to both markets. The authorities might be induced in such a case to exercise pressure on exporting enterprises simply to meet the expanded export demands within the CMEA, particularly if imports from this region were concentrated among economically strategic intermediate inputs. In this case the authorities might override the pre-tax motivation of enterprises to expand exports to the MEs by offering special fiscal exemptions and other preferences for increased exports within the CMEA.

Foreign trade and the macroeconomy

System-determined statistical problems.   With the modifications in economic system, the system-determined statistical problems for macroeconomic analysis of the CPE, discussed in Section 4, either disappear or at least are partially ameliorated. The first problem, regarding the importance of the foreign trade sector as a "sector" of national income, should be reduced in the MPE because the quantitative significance of price equalization will be less and the new exchange rate (the foreign trade multiplier, or commercial exchange rate), aside from most likely being closer to purchasing power parity, will now also have somewhat of a price formation role in the domestic economy.

The second problem, involving the calculation of foreign trade participation ratios, should also be less severe in the MPE, due to the combination of an economically more meaningful exchange rate and domestic prices that are more reflective of real domestic scarcities. Problems may still exist, however, along the lines of the well-known difficulties encountered in international comparisons of the national incomes of developing and developed market economies. It is now widely accepted that the use of official exchange rates may understate the relative incomes of the developing countries, at least when compared to income calculations based on purchasing power parity calculations. The same problem may exist for MPEs as well, because their foreign trade multipliers or commercial exchange rates may be set much higher than justified on purchasing power parity grounds, in an effort to compensate for the relatively low export supply and import demand elasticities alluded to earlier. In other words, whereas the valuta exchange rates may typically overstate the purchasing power of the domestic currencies of CPEs, the commercial exchange rates of MPEs may understate the purchasing power of their local currencies.[52]

Third, the adoption of a foreign trade multiplier or commercial exchange rate by the MPE may have the result of reducing the bias in the reported value of TR-settled trade flows *vis-à-vis* the value of flows settled in convertible currency. MPE authorities, in the interest of strengthening the role of market-determined relative prices in resource allocation, may attempt through exchange rate policy to equate the domestic currency proceeds earned by enterprises in exporting essentially identical goods to the TR and convertible currency areas respectively. To do this they must set the commercial cross rate between the TR and the dollar in such a way as to exactly offset the effect of intra-CMEA foreign trade price distortions converted into TRs at the official CMEA exchange rate (in other words, by setting $e_c = (1 + \alpha)e_i$, in Eq. (9)). This, as can also be seen by Eq. (9), will likewise have the effect of eliminating any conversion bias in the "forwards" conversion of the MPE's trade statistics into dollars. Because the level of the exchange rate *vis-à-vis* the convertible currency area in particular will reflect other policy objectives as well, however, including the desired convertible currency trade balance target, the actual official commercial cross rate selected by the authorities may not be one that eliminates all conversion bias (Wolf [136]).

Internal and external balance. As noted, the modified planned economy is not easy to stylize, and therefore formal modelling of internal-external balance issues in the MPE is particularly difficult. In the MPE, for instance, increased profit orientation on the part of enterprises is emphasized, but as a practical matter profit maximization could hardly be said to characterize enterprise behaviour, particularly with respect to pre-tax profits. Price flexibility is an important systemic objective, but as a practical matter various social policy considerations circumscribe this flexibility, and important price distortions may persist. As a result, certain important intermediate inputs may continue to be allocated by the central

---

[52] The issue of the determination of exchange rates in planned economies and their divergence from purchasing power parity is comprehensively dealt with in Marer [73]. Also see van Brabant [117] and Wolf [130].

authorities, rather than by the market. Wages are effectively regulated jointly by the center and the enterprises, and so forth. The modeller's dilemma is that on the one hand the institutional reality of the MPE may be too complex to model effectively; but if one abstracts from most of these institutional complexities, the resultant model will probably resemble very closely a stylized market economy with price distortions, and it may therefore be of only limited use.

The latter type of model, however, may generate some useful analytical insights, and in several cases has been employed with effect in analyzing problems of internal and external balance in the MPE. Consider, for example, an MPE in which the domestic price of its importable (M) is still administratively fixed, but in which the domestic price of its exportable (X), linked to its foreign currency price by a commercial exchange rate or foreign trade multiplier, moves proportionately with this foreign currency price and with the exchange rate. The importable is consequently subject to full price equalization, but it shall be assumed for simplicity that initially the domestic price of the importable is equal, at the existing exchange rate, to its foreign currency price, and net price equalization taxes as well as the trade balances in foreign and in domestic currencies are equal to zero. Initially, domestic production and consumption are at P_0 and C_0, respectively, in Figure 7.

Now assume that world markets for both composite products are subjected to inflation, but that the foreign currency price of the MPE's importable rises faster than that of its exportable, causing the economy's external terms of trade to deteriorate from q_0 to q_1^*. In the stylized market economy, this change in the external terms of trade would be fully reflected, through international commodity arbitrage, in the internal terms of trade and this would induce enterprises to shift productive resources from exportables into importables, and domestic consumption would shift from importables into exportables. Output would slide to the northwest along the production possibilities frontier FF, and consumption generally would move to the southeast of C_0. Trade volumes in both commodities would be reduced, but after any real balance effects had run their course, and the economy had returned to full stock-flow equilibrium, hoarding would be zero and trade would be balanced in both domestic and foreign currencies.

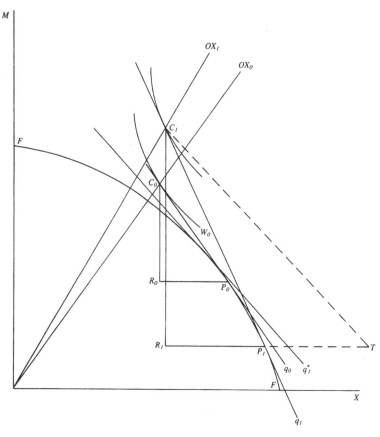

FIGURE 7   The impact of a terms of trade change in a modified planned economy.

In the CPE, as discussed in Section 4, the impact of this external disturbance on the structure of domestic production would probably be minimal, at least in the short- and possibly in the medium term. The effect on domestic consumption of the two tradables would depend, as noted in Sections 3 and 4, on the authorities' tolerance of a deterioration in the valuta trade balance, and on their marginal propensity to (have society) consume the two composite goods. The change in the two trade balances (B_T and B_T') would therefore depend essentially on the authorities' preferences and the availability, in general, of foreign credits.

In the MPE, the impact of this disturbance on resource allocation and the two trade balances will likewise depend on the authorities' response. Avoiding a complete taxonomy here, observe that if the authorities were willing to tolerate a decline in net foreign assets, they might choose to do nothing to offset the domestic and trade balance effects of this particular external disturbance. In that case the deterioration in the external terms of trade would actually result in an improvement of the internal terms of trade (to q_1), because the domestic price of the importable is administratively fixed, while the domestic price of the exportable would rise proportionately to its foreign currency price. This would induce an increase in exportable output at the expense of the importable (to P_1), while consumption would shift towards the now relatively less expensive importable (to C_1). In effect, once consumers and producers had returned to stock-flow equilibrium ($B_T = 0$), trade would have expanded and consumers would have achieved a higher welfare level, but only at the cost of a foreign currency trade deficit (equal to $P_1 T_1$) exactly offset by net price equalization subsidies on the importable ($B'_T = B_T + T$, where $B_T = 0$—see Eq. (8)), and a distortion of domestic prices and therefore of resource allocation. The resulting trade deficit in foreign currency prices would also be larger than that incurred by an otherwise comparable CPE that pursued a policy of fully insulating the domestic economy from the disturbance. In a more complex model with an imported intermediate good, the same type of external disturbance could result, in the MPE, in positive relative effective protection of its export, despite the external terms of trade deterioration.[53]

The foregoing example of an undesired "perverse" reaction to an exogenous disturbance is of course dependent, *inter alia,* on the sensitivity of enterprises in the MPE to changes in relative domestic prices. This sensitivity may, as noted earlier, be dampened for several reasons. Nevertheless, this example does highlight a serious issue for the authorities in a modified planned economy with a partially or wholly decentralized foreign trade system. The problem

---

[53] Such results are not just theoretical oddities. See Wolf [125] for a detailed examination of such a case, and its applicability to one and possibly two planned economies in the aftermath of the first oil price shock in the mid-1970s. Also see Wolf [132] and Böhm [10].

is that many prices remain distorted in the MPE, yet enterprises now may have both the motivation and the autonomy to use efficiently the modified environment to their own, but not necessarily to the economy's, advantage. The tendency of micro- and macro-level interests to coincide, which is a plausible outcome in the stylized market economy with generally flexible prices, cannot necessarily be assumed in the MPE, unless the authorities are able to set, or let the market freely establish, a structure of "correct" prices throughout the economy. The authorities' awareness of this problem, combined with an inability or unwillingness to permit a larger scope for market-determined prices, may lead the authorities to tighten formal and informal controls on enterprise activities, which in effect will move the system back towards that of the CPE.

With the expansion of the scope for market forces, and the intensified organizational and price linkages between foreign trade and the domestic economy in the MPE, considerable attention has recently been focused on the extent to which the exchange rate with respect to convertible currencies could become a significant instrument for macroeconomic stabilization in this economy. The foregoing discussion of the response to external disturbances suggests that in the event that elasticities are more than negligible, and yet the foreign trade sector of the MPE is still characterized by significant price distortions, a change in the exchange rate could well have "perverse" effects in the sense of a real devaluation causing a deterioration in the foreign currency trade balance (Wolf [123, 126]).

This type of perverse response to devaluation (unlike that occasioned in the market economy by nonfulfillment of the Marshall-Lerner condition) depends, as does a positive trade balance impact of devaluation, on the assumption of a non-negligible degree of response by enterprises to a change in the exchange rate. That firms are are likely to respond significantly to a devaluation in the MPE is doubted by many close observers of these economies. This skepticism stems basically from one or more of the following assumptions.

First, it is frequently assumed that a devaluation in a MPE will have little or no effect on domestic relative prices. For instance, if the authorities in their regulation of domestic prices permit the prices of all tradables to rise proportionately with the exchange rate, and the prices of nontradables depend in part on the cost of tradable inputs, then this may be seen as severely restricting the degree to which domestic relative prices can change (Marer [74]). It should be noted, however, that as long as any initial aggregate excess demand is eliminated by the devaluation, and the price level effects of the change in the exchange rate are not fully accommodated by the monetary authorities, then the domestic prices of tradables will increase relative to the prices of non-tradables as the result of the expenditure-reducing effect of devaluation (Wolf [123]). If, on the other hand, the prices of various nontradables are fixed by the authorities, a devaluation will definitely increase the relative price of tradables regardless of the aggregate demand management policy that is pursued.

A second basis for skepticism about the trade balance effects of devaluation derives from the above-mentioned possibility of fixed-price nontradables. While devaluation will lower their relative price, and may encourage a shift in productive resources out of nontradables toward tradables, it will also increase the degree of excess demand for the nontradables and could lead to increased "forced substitution" of tradables for nontradables in domestic consumption, reduced effective labor supply by disgruntled consumers, and so forth—all tending to impede the actual improvement in the trade balance.[54]

Third, it is sometimes argued that real-world MPEs, despite their only negligible shares in world trade, may effectively face downward-sloping demand curves for their exportables in trade with market economies as a group. As a result, an increase in the exchange rate is viewed as causing a deterioration in their terms of trade that might offset much or all of the positive impact of devaluation on export volumes.[55] While a devaluation-induced decline in the terms of trade is plausible for even small-sized MPEs, it should also be recognized that to the extent it does occur, the

---

[54] See Wolf [138]. The notion of "forced substitution" is from Kornai [63].

[55] Holzman [54] discusses reasons why the demand of market economies for the exportables of planned economies may be relatively price inelastic. Although that discussion mainly concerns CPEs, it is often applied to MPEs as well. Some empirical estimates of the elasticity of ME demand with respect to the relative price of Hungarian exports is provided in Botos and Riecke [15] and Tarafas and Szabo [108]; a critical evaluation of these estimates appears in Wolf [137].

domestic price level impact of devaluation, which is often considered to be a negative effect, will be correspondingly weakened. Moreover, although a deterioration in the terms of trade does involve a loss in real income, it also means a worsening of the trade balance only in the event that the economy is actually operating in the inelastic (in other words, less than unit elastic) range of its export demand curve (Wolf [137]).

Fourth, if most or all of the MPE's trade settled for transferable rubles is not, as a practical matter, substitutable in the short-run for tradables sold to the convertible currency area, then this trade would constitute a so-called ruble core of tradables that is largely unaffected by devaluation. This would tend to reduce the expenditure-reducing effect of devaluation on the convertible currency trade balance, because the decline in domestic real expenditure on the "ruble core" goods, induced by the price level effect of devaluation, would lead either to a short-run surplus in TR trade or to excessive inventory accumulation of TR-settled products, rather than to increased net exports of these goods to the convertible currency area (Wolf [138]).

A final argument, however, may be the most persuasive regarding the ineffectiveness (at least relative to the stylized ME) of devaluation in the modified planned economy. According to this view, devaluation may lack effectiveness not so much because of rigid relative prices, effects of disequilibrium, inelastic export demand, or low substitutability between ruble and non-ruble exports, but because MPE enterprises are not subjected to financial discipline (i.e., have a soft budget constraint), they discover that extraordinary profits earned through taking advantage of devaluation may be confiscated, and they are frequently subject to informal pressures from the authorities to provide adequate supplies of various products to domestic markets at artificially low prices (Kornai [64, 65, 66] and Tardos [109]). Significant constraints on labor and capital mobility in the short-run may also be viewed as lowering, in general, the effective supply elasticities of MPE enterprises (Wolf [138]).

That domestic supply elasticities and possibly demand elasticities within the enterprise sector (with respect to changes in relative prices) may well be lower in the MPE than in otherwise comparable market economies, is quite plausible. It should be emphasized, however, that existing price elasticities, as well as the responsiveness of domestic expenditure to devaluation, are in reality not completely exogenous parameters beyond the influence of the authorities. Indeed, the sensitivity of real aggregate expenditure with respect to devaluation is in theory very much under their influence. Regardless of the particular institutional structure of the domestic financial system, it is the authorities who ultimately can control the extension of credit to the economy as well as the degree of financial discipline imposed on enterprises. The various "price elasticities" are also subject to influence by the authorities, to some extent even in the short run, through policies that enforce hard budget constraints and avoid the conveying of non-price signals to enterprises.[56] Over the medium and longer term, measures aimed at expanding domestic factor mobility and reducing the pervasive intervention by the authorities that limits the autonomy of enterprises, would also presumably tend to raise the trade elasticities of the modified planned economy.

6. SUMMARY

The foreign trade of centrally planned economies (CPEs) in Eastern Europe and the Soviet Union is decisively determined by the economic system of the CPE and by the particular set of policy objectives pursued by the authorities in these economies. Policy objectives of particular significance for the conduct of foreign trade and its impact on the domestic economy have included the rigidity of domestic producer and consumer prices, full employment and job security, and rapid industrialization and economic growth.

As discussed in some detail in Section 2, the combination of a centrally planned and administered economic system and these policy objectives has caused the foreign trade of CPEs to be subordinated to fulfillment of the national economic plan and provision of domestic economic stability. Centrally planned economies consequently have a tendency to trade less than otherwise comparable market economies (MEs), and to place much less

---

[56] The institutional and policy environment that constrains the authorities in this regard is discussed in detail in Kornai [66] and Marer [74].

emphasis on the narrow economic efficiency of foreign trade. The relative neglect of foreign trade and its efficiency, combined with the fundamental separation of domestic enterprises from foreign markets, as well as other factors, result in CPEs being at a competitive disadvantage in selling higher quality finished and semi-finished manufactures on world markets. Although foreign trade, with both other CPEs and market economies, has served to provide centrally planned economies with a wide range of needed inputs for national plan fulfillment, it has not played a particularly dynamic role in the development of these economies.

As a result of the fundamental separation of domestic enterprises and the internal price system from foreign trade in the CPE, the issue of what and how much to trade with the outside world has been a difficult and continuing preoccupation of policymakers and economists in these countries. Section 3 examined many of the obstacles encountered in attempting to enhance the efficiency of foreign trade decisionmaking in the centrally planned economy; one of these obstacles is an exchange rate which typically has only an accounting rather than an economic function.

The trade offer curve of the CPE was portrayed in Section 3 as having a backward bending shape, in contrast to the positive sloping offer curve usually assumed for the market economy with its profit-oriented autonomous enterprises engaged in foreign trade. Thus the central planners, who are assumed here to be virtually totally insensitive to changes in relative prices in the domestic allocation of resources, would be expected to increase rather than decrease export volumes in the event of a deterioration in the terms of trade, in order to alleviate somewhat the need to reduce the volume of imports critical to national plan fulfillment. The peculiarities of the CPE offer curve have some particular implications for the conduct of foreign trade with market economies. Trade among centrally planned economies is characterized as well by a number of specific features—including the distinction between "hard" and "soft" goods, the prevalence of bilateralism, and a number of possibilities for arbitrage—that are generally lacking in trade among market economies.

The insulation of the structure and level of domestic prices, and the lack of economic significance of the exchange rate in CPEs, significantly complicate analysis of the role of foreign trade in aggregate economic activity and in the process of macroeconomic adjustment in centrally planned economies. This issue was addressed in Section 4, together with the problem of achieving both internal and external macroeconomic balance in these economies. Although the same basic analytical framework can be used to study macroeconomic processes in CPEs as in market economies, the existence of the price equalization system and the pervasive central administration of economic activity means that many of the natural "equilibrating" activities of autonomous economic agents, assumed in analyses of the stylized ME, cannot be presumed to operate in the CPE. To the degree that equilibrating adjustments do take place, however, they are more likely to reflect quantity rather than price changes in the CPE. The response of the CPE to an exogenous real disturbance in foreign trade would typically be different from that encountered in the market economy. In the latter, for example, a deterioration in the terms of trade may have a deflationary effect, whereas its short- or medium-term impact in the CPE is more likely to be inflationary.

As economic development has proceeded in the CPEs, the scope has diminished for further rapid growth based on an *extensive* strategy emphasizing the accumulation of productive factors. At the same time, the vast planning and administrative apparatus has become less suited to the direction of the increasingly complex economy. Attention has shifted to the necessity of emphasizing *intensive* development, which involves increasing the productivity of the factors of productions as well as raising the quality of the output of goods and services. The greater stress on efficiency has led to continuing experiments with economic reform, and this has generally included a more determined effort to improve the efficiency of foreign trade decisionmaking.

Two basic types of reform may be distinguished. One involves attempts to "improve" or "perfect" the system of central planning, without changing the basic character of the economic system. The other approach consists of a more comprehensive and market-oriented reform, involving changes which may lead to a "modified planned economy" (MPE). This latter reform approach was discussed in some detail in Section 5, particularly insofar as it affects the system and practice of foreign trade. In principle, a pronounced movement toward a more market-oriented economic system has significant implications for foreign trade decisionmaking at the micro level, as well as for the role of foreign trade in the macroeconomy.

Because the MPE is a hybrid combining some continuing features of central planning and emerging market relationships, policymaking regarding foreign trade in this economy becomes, as a practical matter, quite complex. The granting of greater autonomy to enterprises, in an increasingly marketized economy, threatens the dominant role of the governmental bureaucratic apparatus in the direction of the economy. Because many prices remain distorted in the MPE, the tendency of micro- and macro-level interests to coincide, which is a plausible outcome in the stylized ME with generally flexible prices, cannot necessarily be taken for granted in the MPE. Moreover, the authorities will face strong pressures to protect weak enterprises as well as households (in their roles of both income earners and consumers), from the economic uncertainties caused by unrestrained enterprise responses to market forces unleashed by the reform.

Awareness of these difficulties may lead the authorities to retain much of their scope for intervention in enterprise activities, although in the modified environment this may be achieved more through the use of differentiated financial incentives and fiscal redistribution than by direct, administrative controls. In foreign trade, as in the rest of economic activity, the authorities in the MPE face the difficult challenge of achieving greater efficiency and economic dynamism in an institutional, social and political environment that continues in effect to pose significant obstacles to such improvements.

Acknowledgement

The author would like to thank J. Michael Montias for his encouragement to write this monograph, and for his critical comments on earlier versions.

References

References marked with a single asterisk denote works essential to an understanding of the field, to which the reader should turn first for a deeper knowledge of the topics covered in this survey. Those marked with a double asterisk are mentioned in the text but are not so basic to the field.

[1] Allen, M. (1976) The Structure and Reform of the Exchange and Payments Systems of Some East European Countries. *Staff Papers,* International Monetary Fund, **23, 718–739.

[2] Allen, M. (1982) Adjustment in Planned Economies. *Staff Papers,* International Monetary Fund, **29,** 398–421.

[3] Allen, R. L. (1958) Economic Motives in Soviet Foreign Trade Policy. *Southern Economic Journal,* **25,** 189–201.

[4] Ames, E. (1965) *Soviet Economic Processes.* Homewood, Ill.: Richard D. Irwin.

**[5] Ausch, S. (1972) *Theory and Practice of CMEA Cooperation.* Budapest: Akademiai Kiado.

[6] Balassa, B. (1983) Reforming the New Economic Mechanism in Hungary. *Journal of Comparative Economics,* **7,** 253–276.

[7] Batra, R. N. (1976) The Theory of International Trade with an International Cartel or a Centrally Planned Economy. *Southern Economic Journal,* **42, 364–376.

[8] Bauer, T. (1983) The Hungarian Alternative to Soviet-Type Planning. *Journal of Comparative Economics,* **7, 304–316.

[9] Bergson, A. (1980) The Geometry of COMECON Trade. *European Economic Review,* **14, 291–306.

[10] Böhm, E. (1983) Die Wechselkurse in polnischen Westhandel, 1971–1982. *Osteuropa Wirtschaft,* **28, 204–216.

[11] Böhm, E. (1986) *Wechselkurspolitik in der Planwirtschaft.* Hamburg: Verlag Weltarchiv.

*[12] Boltho, A. (1971) *Foreign Trade Criteria in Socialist Economies.* London: Cambridge University Press.

**[13] Bornstein, M. (1977) Economic Reform in Eastern Europe. In *East European Economies Post-Helsinki,* Joint Economic Committee, U.S. Congress, pp. 102–134. Washington, D.C.: U.S. Government Printing Office.

**[14] Bornstein, M. (1980) Systemic Aspects of the Responses of East European Economies to Disturbances in the International Economy. In *The Impact of International Economic Disturbances on the Soviet Union and Eastern Europe,* edited by E. Neuberger and L. D. Tyson, pp. 308–320. New York: Pergamon.

[15] Botos, K. and W. Riecke (1985) Einige Fragen der ungarischen Wechselkurspolitik. *Osteuropa Wirtschaft,* **30, 181–188.

[16] Brada, J. C. (1973) The Microallocative Impact of the Hungrian Economic Reform of 1968: Some Evidence from the Export Sector. *Economics of Planning,* **13,** 1–14.

[17] Brada, J. C. (1976) *Quantitative and Analytical Studies in East-West Economic Relations.* Bloomington, Ind.: IDRC, Indiana University.

[18] Brada, J. C. (1982) Real and Monetary Approaches to Foreign Trade Adjustment Mechanisms in Centrally Planned Economies. *European Economic Review,* **19, 229–244.

[19] Brada, J. C. (1983) The Soviet-American Grain Agreement and the National Interest. *American Journal of Agricultural Economics,* **19, 651–656.

[20] Brada, J. C. (1985) Soviet Subsidization of Eastern Europe: The Primacy of Economics over Politics? *Journal of Comparative Economics,* **9, 80–92.

[21] Brada, J. C. and M. R. Jackson (1978) The Organization of Foreign Trade Under Capitalism and Socialism. *Journal of Comparative Economics,* **2, 293–320.

[22] Brada, J. C., E. A. Hewett, and T. A. Wolf (1988) *Economic Adjustment and Reform in Eastern Europe and the Soviet Union: Essays in Honor of Franklyn D. Holzman.* Durham, N.C.: Duke Univ. Press.

**[23] Brainard, L. J. (1980) CMEA Financial System and Integration. In *East European Integration and East-West Trade*, edited by P. Marer and J. M. Montias, pp. 121–138. Bloomington, Ind.: Indiana University Press.

*[24] Brown, A. A. (1968) Towards a Theory of Centrally Planned Foreign Trade. In *International Trade and Central Planning*, edited by A. A. Brown and E. Neuberger, pp. 57–93. Berkeley: University of California Press.

**[25] Brown, A. A. and P. Marer (1973) Foreign Trade in the East European Reforms. In *Plan and Market*, edited by M. Bornstein, pp. 153–205. New Haven: Yale University Press.

*[26] Brown, A. A. and E. Neuberger (1968) *International Trade and Central Planning.* Berkeley: University of California Press.

**[27] Campbell, R. W. (1974) *The Soviet-Type Economies.* Boston: Houghton Mifflin.

**[28] Dietz, R. (1986) Advantages and Disadvantages in Soviet Trade with Eastern Europe, The Pricing Dimension. In *East European Economies: Slow Growth in the 1980s, 2*, Joint Economic Committee, U.S. Congress, pp. 263–301. Washington, D.C.: U.S. Government Printing Office.

[29] Dietz, R. (1986) Soviet Foregone Gains in Trade with the CMEA Six: A Reappraisal. *Comparative Economic Studies*, **28, 69–94.

[30] Ellis, H. S. (1945) Bilateralism and the Future of International Trade. *Essays in International Finance*, **5.

[31] Fink, G. (1984) Verrechnungssystem und Hartwährungshandel in RGW, Sudosteuropa. *Zeitschrift fur Gegenwartsforschung*, **33, 341–351.

**[32] Foldi, T. and T. Kiss (1969) *Socialist World Market Prices.* Leyden: Sijthoff.

[33] Gardner, H. S. (1979) The Factor Content of Soviet Foreign Trade: A Synthesis. *ACES Bulletin*, **21, 1–16.

[34] Gardner, H. S. (1981) The Embodied Factor Content of Soviet Foreign Trade: A Rejoinder. *ACES Bulletin*, **23, 89–101.

*[35] Gardner, H. S. (1983) *Soviet Foreign Trade: The Decision Process.* Boston: Kluwer-Nijhoff,

**[36] Gruzinov, V. P. (1979) *The USSR's Management of Foreign Trade.* White Plains: M. E. Sharpe.

*[37] Hewett, E. A. (1974) *Foreign Trade Prices in the Council for Mutual Economic Assistance.* London: Cambridge University Press.

**[38] Hewett, E. A. (1976) A Gravity Model of CMEA Trade. In *Quantitative and Analytical Studies in East-West Economic Relations*, edited by J. C. Brada, pp. 1–15. Bloomington, Ind.: IDRC, Indiana University.

**[39] Hewett, E. A. (1976) A Model of Foreign Trade Planning in an Eastern European-Type Economy. In *Economic Analysis of the Soviet-Type System*, edited by J. Thornton, pp. 156–175. London: Cambridge University Press.

*[40] Hewett, E. A. (1977) Prices and Resource Allocation in Intra-CMEA Trade. In *The Socialist Price Mechanism*, edited by A. Abouchar, pp. 95–128. Durham, N.C.: Duke University Press.

[41] Hewett, E. A. (1978) Most-Favoured Nation Treatment in Trade Under Central Planning. *Slavic Review*, **37, 25–39.

*[42] Hewett, E. A. (1980) Foreign Trade Outcomes in Eastern and Western Economies. In *East European Integration and East-West Trade*, edited by P. Marer and J. M. Montias, pp. 41–69. Bloomington, Ind.: Indiana University Press.

[43] Hewett, E. A. (1983) Foreign Economic Relations. In *The Soviet Economy*: *Toward the Year 2000*, edited by A. Bergson and H. S. Levine, pp. 269–310. London: Allen & Unwin.

[44] Holzman, F. D. (1953) The Profit-Output Relationship of a Soviet Firm: Comment. *Canadian Journal of Economics and Political Science*, **19, 523–531.

[45] Holzman, F. D. (1962) Soviet Foreign Trade Pricing and the Question of Discrimination: A 'Customs Union' Approach. *Review of Economics and Statistics*, **54, 134–147.

[46] Holzman, F. D. (1965) More on Soviet Bloc Trade Discrimination. *Soviet Studies*, **17, 44–65.

*[47] Holzman, F. D. (1966) Foreign Trade Behavior of Centrally Planned Economies. In *Industrialization in Two Systems: Essays in Honor of Alexander Gerschenkron*, edited by H. Rosovsky, pp. 237–263. New York: Wiley.

*[48] Holzman, F. D. (1968) Soviet Central Planning and Its Impact on Foreign Trade Behavior and Adjustment Mechanisms. In *International Trade and Central Planning*, edited by A. A. Brown and E. Neuberger, pp. 280–305. Berkeley: University of California Press, 1968.

*[49] Holzman, F. D. (1974) *Foreign Trade Under Central Planning*. Cambridge, Mass: Harvard University Press.

**[50] Holzman, F. D. (1974) Foreign Trade GNP Accounting Methodology in Centrally Planned and Capitalist Economies. *Journal of International Economics*, 59–66.

**[51] Holzman, F. D. (1974) Import Bottlenecks and the Foreign Trade Multiplier. In *Foreign Trade Under Central Planning*, edited by F. D. Holzman, pp. 126–135. Cambridge, Mass.: Harvard University Press.

**[52] Holzman, F. D. (1976) *International Trade Under Communism*. New York: Basic Books.

**[53] Holzman, F. D. (1978) CMEA's Hard Currency Deficits and Convertibility. In *Economic Relations Between East and West*, edited by N. G. M. Watts. pp. 144–163. New York: St. Martin's Press.

**[54] Holzman, F. D. (1979) Some Theories of the Hard Currency Shortages of Centrally Planned Economies. In *Soviet Economy in a Time of Change*, Washington, D.C.: U.S. Government Printing Office.

**[55] Holzman, F. D. (1980) Comments. In *The Impact of International Economic Disturbances on the Soviet Union and Eastern Europe*, edited by E. Neuberger and L. D. Tyson, pp. 113–118, New York: Pergamon.

[56] Holzman, F. D. (1985) Comecon: A 'Trade Destroying' Customs Union? *Journal of Comparative Economics*, **9, 410–423.

[57] Holzman, F. D. (1986) The Significance of Soviet Subsidies to Eastern Europe. *Comparative Economic Studies*, **28, 54–65.

[58] Hunter, H. (1961) Optimum Tautness in Developmental Planning. *Economic Development and Cultural Change*, **9, 561–572.

**[59] Kaser, M. (1967). *Comecon*. London: Oxford University Press.

[60] Kiss, T. (1973). *The Market of Socialist Economic Integration*. Budapest: Akademiai Kiado.

**[61] Koopmans, T. C. and J. M. Montias (1971) On the Description and Comparison of Economic Systems. In *Comparison of Economic Systems*, edited by A. Eckstein, pp. 27–78. Berkeley: University of California Press.

**[62] Kornai, J. (1976) Pressure and Suction on the Market. In *Economic Analysis* *of the Soviet Type System*, edited by J. Thornton, pp. 191–215. London: Cambridge University Press.

[63] Kornai, J. (1979) Resource-Constrained versus Demand-Constrained Systems. *Econometrica*, **47, 801–819.

**[64] Kornai, J. (1980) *Economics of Shortage*, 2 vols. Amsterdam: North-Holland.

[65] Kornai, J. (1982) Adjustment to Price and Quantity Signals in the Socialist Economy. *Economie Appliquée*, **35(3), 503–524.

[66] Kornai, J. (1986) The Hungarian Reform Process: Visions, Hopes and Reality", *Journal of Economic Literature*, **24, 1687–1737.

[67] Kostecki, M. M. (1983) *The Soviet Impact on Commodity Markets*. London: Macmillan.

[68] Koves, A. (1983) Implicit Subsidies and Some Issues of Economic Relations Within the CMEA. *Acta Oeconomica*, **31, 125–136.

[69] Lawson, C. W. (1974) An Empirical Analysis of the Structure and Stability of Communist Foreign Trade, 1960–1968. *Soviet Studies*, **26, 224–238.

**[70] Lawson, C. W. and P. Wiles (1980) The Soviet-Type Economy as a Generator of Economic Disturbances. In *The Impact of International Economic Disturbances on the Soviet Union and Eastern Europe*, edited by E. Neuberger and L. D. Tyson, pp. 349–374. New York: Pergamon.

**[71] Marer, P. (1972) *Postwar Pricing and Price Patterns in Socialist Foreign Trade, 1946–1971*. Bloomington, Ind.: IDRC, Indiana University.

**[72] Marer, P. (1984) The Political Economy of Soviet Relations with Eastern Europe. In *Soviet Policy in Eastern Europe*, edited by S. M. Terry, pp. 155–188. New Haven: Yale University Press.

**[73] Marer, P. (1985) *Dollar GNPs of the U.S.S.R and Eastern Europe*. Baltimore: Johns Hopkins University Press.

**[74] Marer, P. (1986) Economic Reform in Hungary: From Central Planning to Regulated Market. In *East European Economies: Slow Growth in the 1980s*, vol. 3, Joint Economic Committee, U.S. Congress, pp. 223–297. Washington, D.C.: U.S. Government Printing Office.

*[75] Marer, P. and J. M. Montias, (1980) Theory and Measurement of East European Integration. In *East European Integration and East-West Trade*, edited by P. Marer and J. M. Montias, pp. 3–38. Bloomington, Ind.: Indiana University Press.

*[76] Marer, P. and J. M. Montias, (1980) *East European Integration and East-West Trade*. Bloomington, Ind.: Indiana University Press.

*[77] Marrese, M. and J. Vanous (1983) *Soviet Subsidization of Trade with Eastern Europe*. Berkeley: University of California Press.

[78] Marrese, M. and J. Vanous (1983) Unconventional Gains from Trade. *Journal of Comparative Economics*, **7, 382–399.

**[79] Marrese, M. and J. Vanous (1988) The Content and Controversy of Soviet Trade Relations with Eastern Europe, 1970–84. In *Economic Adjustment and Reform in Eastern Europe and the Soviet Union: Essays in Honor of Franklyn D. Holzman*, edited by J. C. Brada, E. A. Hewett and T. A. Wolf. Durham, N.C.: Duke University Press.

[80] McMillan, C. H. (1973) Factor Proportions and Structure of Soviet Foreign Trade. *ACES Bulletin*, **15, 57–81.

[81] McMillan, C. H. (1974) More on the Factor Content of Soviet Trade. *ACES Bulletin*, **16, 56–58.

**[82] Mendershausen, H. (1959) Terms of Trade Between the Soviet Union and

Smaller Communist Countries, *Review of Economics and Statistics*, **41**, 106–118.
[83] Mendershausen, H. (1960) The Terms of Trade of Soviet-Satellite Trade: A Broadened Analysis, *Review of Economics and Statistics*, **52, 152–163.
**[84] Montias, J. M. (1976) *The Structure of Economic Systems*. New Haven: Yale University Press.
**[85] Montias, J. M. (1976) Socialist Industrialization and Trade in Manufactures. In *Quantitative and Analytical Studies in East-West Economic Relations*, edited by J. C. Brada. Bloomington, Ind.: IDRC, Indiana University.
**[86] Myint, H. (1958) The 'Classical Theory' of International Trade and the Underdeveloped Countries. *Economic Journal*, 317–337.
[87] Neuberger, E. (1964) Is the USSR Superior to the West as a Market for Primary Products?, *Review of Economics and Statistics*, **46, 287–293.
[88] Neuberger, E. (1964) International Division of Labor in CEMA: Limited Regret Strategy. *American Economic Review, Papers and Proceedings*, **54, 506–515.
*[89] Neuberger, E. and L. D. Tyson (1980) *The Impact of International Economic Disturbances on the Soviet Union and Eastern Europe*. New York: Pergamon, 1980.
**[90] Nove, A. (1977) *The Soviet Economic System*. London: Allen & Unwin.
[91] Nove, A. (1986) Some Statistical Puzzles Examined. *Soviet Studies*, **38, 98–102.
**[92] Pécsi, K. (1981) *The Future of Socialist Economic Integration*. Armonk, N.Y.: M.E. Sharpe.
[93] Plowiec, U. (1973–74) Trends Toward Improving the Workings of Poland's Foreign Trade. *Soviet and East European Foreign Trade*, **9, 42–71.
*[94] Portes, R. (1979) Internal and External Balance in a Centrally Planned Economy. *Journal of Comparative Economics*, **3**, 325–345.
*[95] Portes, R. (1984) The Theory and Measurement of Macroeconomic Disequilibrium in Centrally Planned Economies. Paper presented at the Conference on the Soviet Union and Eastern Europe in the World Economy, Washington, D.C., October 1984.
*[96] Pryor, F. L. (1963) *The Communist Foreign Trade System*. Cambridge, Mass.: MIT Press.
**[97] Rosefielde, S. (1973) *Soviet International Trade in Heckscher–Ohlin Perspective*. Lexington, Mass.: Lexington Books.
[98] Rosefielde, S. (1973) The Embodied Factor Content of Soviet International Trade: Problems of Theory, Measurement and Interpretation. *ACES Bulletin*, **15, 3–12.
[99] Rosefielde, S. (1974) Factor Proportions and Economic Rationality in Soviet International Trade. *American Economic Review*, **64, 670–681.
[100] Rosefielde, S. (1976) Foreign Trade Prices and the Heckscher-Ohlin Interpretation of Soviet Foreign Trade. *ACES Bulletin*, **18, 31–38.
[101] Rosefielde, S. (1979) Is the Embodied Factor Content of Soviet Foreign Trade Hyper-Irrational? *ACES Bulletin*, **21, 19–51.
**[102] Rosefielde, S. (1981) Comparative Advantage and the Evolving Pattern of Soviet International Commodity Specialization, 1950–1973. In *Economic Welfare and the Economics of Soviet Socialism*, edited by S. Rosefielde. London: Cambridge University Press.
[103] Rostowski, J. and Auerbach, P. (1986) Storming Cycles and Economic Systems. *Journal of Comparative Economics*, **10, 293–312.

**[104] Shagalov, G. L. (1973) *Problemy Optimal'nogo planirovaniia vneshne-ekonomicheskikh sviazei.* Moscow: Nauka.

**[105] Shagalov, G. L. (1983) *Effektivnost' ekonomicheskogo sotrudnichestva stran CEV.* Moscow: Ekonomika.

**[106] Shagalov, G. L. and D. S. Faermark (1981) Povyshenie effektivnosti i optimizatsiia vneshneekonomicheskikh sviazei otrasli. In *Voprosy optimizatsii i prognizorovaniia vneshnei torgovli,* edited by G. L. Shagalov, pp. 4–22. Moscow: TsEMI.

[107] Staller, G. J. (1967) Patterns of Stability in Foreign Trade: OECD and COMECON, 1950–1963. *American Economic Review,* **57, 879–888.

[108] Tarafas, I and J. Szabo (1985) Hungary's Exchange Rate Policy in the 1980s. *Acta Oeconomica,* **35, 53–79.

[109] Tardos, M. (1980) The Role of Money: Economic Relations Between the State and the Enterprises in Hungary, *Acta Oeconomica,* **25, 19–35.

**[110] Tardos, M. (1988) How to Create Markets in Eastern Europe: The Hungarian Case. In *Economic Adjustment and Reforms in Eastern Europe and the Soviet Union: Essays in Honor of Franklyn D. Holzman,* edited by J. C. Brada, E. A. Hewett and T. A. Wolf. Durham, N.C.: Duke University Press.

**[111] Treml, V. G. (1983) Soviet Dependence on Foreign Trade. In *External Economic Relations of CMEA Countries.* Brussels: NATO.

**[112] Treml, V. G. and Kostinsky, B. L. (1982) *The Domestic Value of Soviet Foreign Trade: Exports and Imports in the 1972 Input-Output Table.* Washington, D.C.: U.S. Bureau of the Census.

[113] Trzeciakowski, W. (1962) Model optymalizacjii bieżacej handlu zagranicznego i jego zastosowanie. *Przeglad Statystyczny,* **2.

*[114] Trzeciakowski, W. (1978) *Indirect Management in a Centrally Planned Economy.* Amsterdam: North Holland.

*[115] van Brabant, J. M. P. (1973) *Bilateralism and Structural Bilateralism in Intra-CMEA Trade.* Rotterdam: Rotterdam University Press.

[116] van Brabant, J. M. P. (1977) The Relationship Between Domestic and Foreign Trade Prices in Centrally Planned Economies: The Case of Hungary. *Osteuropa Wirtschaft,* **22,** 235–258.

**[117] van Brabant, J. M. P. (1985) Exchange Rates in Eastern Europe: Types, Derivation and Application. *World Bank Staff Working Paper* No. 778. Washington, D.C.: World Bank.

[118] van Brabant, J. M. P. (1985) The Relationship Between World and Socialist Trade Prices—Some Empirical Evidence. *Journal of Comparative Economics,* **9, 233–251.

[119] Wilczynski, J. (1969) *The Economics and Politics of East-West Trade.* New York: Praeger.

*[120] Wiles, P. J. D. (1968) *Communist International Economics.* New York: Praeger.

[121] Winiecki, J. (1986) Central Planning and Export Orientation. *Eastern European Economics,* **24, 67–89.

[122] Wolf, T. A. (1978) The Theory of International Trade with an International Cartel or a Centrally Planned Economy: Comment. *Southern Economic Journal,* **44, 987–991.

[123] Wolf, T. A. (1978) Exchange Rate Adjustments in Small Market and Centrally Planned Economies. *Journal of Comparative Economics,* **2, 226–245.

*[124] Wolf, T. A. (1980) On the Adjustment of Centrally Planned Economies to External Economic Disturbances. In *East European Integration and East-West Trade*, edited by P. Marer and J. M. Montias, pp. 86–111. Bloomington, Ind.: Indiana University Press.

**[125] Wolf, T. A. (1980) External Inflation, the Balance of Trade, and Resource Allocation in Small Centrally Planned Economies. In *The Impact of International Economic Disturbances on the Soviet Union and Eastern Europe*, edited by E. Neuberger and L. D. Tyson. pp. 63–87. New York: Pergamon.

**[126] Wolf, T. A. (1980) Devaluation in 'Large' Modified Centrally Planned Economies. *Journal of Comparative Economics, 4*, 415–419.

*[127] Wolf, T. A. (1982) Optimal Foreign Trade for the Price-Insensitive Soviet-Type Economy. *Journal of Comparative Economics, 6*, 37–54.

**[128] Wolf, T. A. (1982) Soviet Market Power and Pricing Behavior in Western Export Markets. *Soviet Studies, 34*, 529–546.

**[129] Wolf, T. A. (1983) East-West Trade: Economic Interests, Systemic Interaction and Political Rivalry, *ACES Bulletin, 25*, 23–59.

**[130] Wolf, T. A. (1985) Exchange Rates, Foreign Trade Accounting and Purchasing Power Parity for Centrally Planned Economies. *World Bank Staff Working Paper*, No. 779. Washington, D.C.: World Bank.

*[131] Wolf, T. A. (1985) Economic Stabilization in Planned Economies: Toward an Analytical Framework. *Staff Papers*, International Monetary Fund, *32*, 78–131.

*[132] Wolf, T. A. (1985) Exchange Rate Systems and Adjustment in Planned Economies. *Staff Papers*, International Monetary Fund, *32*, 211–247.

**[133] Wolf, T. A. (1985) An Empirical Analysis of Soviet Economic Relations with Developing Countries. *Soviet Economy, 1*, 232–260.

**[134] Wolf, T. A. (1985) Estimating 'Foregone Gains' in Soviet-East European Foreign Trade: A Methodological Note. *Comparative Economic Studies, 27*, 83–98.

**[135] Wolf, T. A. (1987) Foreign Trade and National Income Statistics in the Soviet Union. *Soviet Studies, 39*, 122–128.

**[136] Wolf, T. A. (1987) On the Conversion of Ruble Trade Flows into Dollars. *Journal of Comparative Economics, 11*, 558–571.

**[137] Wolf, T. A. (1988) The Simultaneity of the Effects of Devaluation: Implications for Modified Planned Economies. *Acta Oeconomica*.

**[138] Wolf, T. A. (1988) Devaluation in Modified Planned Economies: A Preliminary Model for Hungary. In *Economic Adjustment and Reform in Eastern Europe and the Soviet Union: Essays in Honor of Franklyn D. Holzman*, edited by J. C. Brada, E. A. Hewett and T. A. Wolf. Durham, N.C.: Duke University Press.

**[139] Zakharov, S. N. and G. L. Shagalov (1982) Metody opredeleniia effektivnosti vneshneekonomicheskikh sviazei. *Ekonomia i matematicheskoe metody*, *18*, 1018–1029.

INDEX

For Product Safety Concerns and Information please contact our EU
representative GPSR@taylorandfrancis.com Taylor & Francis Verlag GmbH,
Kaufingerstraße 24, 80331 München, Germany

Printed and bound by CPI Group (UK) Ltd, Croydon, CR0 4YY
08/05/2025
01864488-0001